Inside the Mind of a Marine Drill Instructor

Kevin McDugle

www.TotalPublishingAndMedia.com

Paperback ISBN 978-1-937829-93-3
Hardcover ISBN 978-1-63302-013-9

Contents

Acknowledgements

If I listed every individual who deserved to be listed in this book there would not be enough pages to contain them. I would like to first of all acknowledge and thank the first military men I ever new my father Norman McDugle who served in the US Army and my grandfather Charles Oliver McDugle who served in the US Army under General Patton.

As a drill instructor I would like to dedicate this book to every recruit I ever trained and to those Drill Instructors I served with and those who put me through hell my Senior Drill Instructor SSGT Ray, DI SSGT Borger, DI SGT Steel, DI SGT Brown all with Platoon 2054 of San Diego in 1988.

My daughter Kylie McDugle is the reason I left the Marine Corps and I want her to know I love her one more time than she loves me forever, amen. You do have Marine blood in you.

To my wife Tosha who is one of the best mothers I know and a dang good wife. To my two boys Kaje and Kael may both of you be as blessed as I have been in my life. Thank you for carrying on the McDugle name.

To Drew Stanley, Aubrey Stanley, Corey Colwell and Dylan Colwell all who have had to suffer at being my step kids.

To my mom and dad Norman and Nova McDugle, forgive me for the language in the book you told me to write it the way it was and I think most Marines will know that I cleaned it up quite a bit.

To Soldierswish.org and those who work so hard at granting wishes for those who have sacrificed so much for the greatest country in the world the United States of America.

Thank you Tony Orlando and Colonel Oliver North for continuing to serve our military and for setting a great example for the rest of us to follow.

Semper Fi to all of you especially the Marines and God Bless America!

Foreword by Tony Orlando

Inside the Mind of a Marine Drill Instructor is a book that takes you through the heart, mind, body and soul of an United States Marine Drill Instructor who truly loves his country and God. I have personally witnessed just a few seconds of this drill instructor treating me like a Marine recruit, and I still shudder at the thought of having to live 90 days of boot camp as a Marine recruit. So step inside the mind of Marine Drill Instructor, Sergeant McDugle, and you will gain a new respect for all Marines. This book is a literary wish come true - Tony Orlando.

Introduction

For over 238 years of romp stompin', death dealing destruction, you would rather pack an alligators butt with dynamite than to mess with the corps. Marine Corps Drill Instructors have trained the meanest, most disciplined gutsy fighting machine the world has ever known, the US Marine. Every Marine has had nightmares about their DI. Some are loved and others are hated but all of them made Marines. Stories have been told for years about the legendary Marine Drill Instructor. They are physically fit, well disciplined, with razor creases, and eyeballs that can cut your soul when they look your way. A Marine Drill Instructor can run farther, move faster and fight longer than any other drill instructor because his mind is strong. The Germans called Marines Teufelshunden (Devil Dog) at the battle of Belleau Wood. A Marine Drill Instructor may choke you or spit in your face but everything he does is for a purpose. DI's make Marines out of some of the nastiest god forsaken excuse for humans you have ever seen. The German's called him Devil Dog, his real name is Marine.

The First Twenty-Four

"Yo, sir, can I tell you a joke?"

I stared at the recruit, amazed he would dare to approach me with such informality. He registered no awareness of the hornet's nest he'd just stirred up.

It took me three hours to make a shamble of their squad bay. I dumped over footlockers and tore blankets off their racks; issued boots and clothing went flying. Choice words went flying. I had a storehouse that never ran out.

His fellow recruits paid dearly for his mistake. The whole bunch appeared to be lazy and insolent, so I figured they deserved it.

I confronted each one of them; eyes bulging with red veins, garlic and coffee laced breath scattering the beads of sweat on their faces, my spit spotting their collars, a few peed their pants. Others looked ready to. They got the whole McDugle, up close and personal. Their day had begun—however bright it had looked earlier—it was going to end in hell.

"Recruit!" I hollered. A dark-green was struggling with his rack; the one I'd torn apart moments earlier.

"SIR, YES SIR!"

"Get that rack in order. ARE YOU OUT OF YOUR FUCKING MIND?"

"SIR, YES SIR!" "I FIGURED YOU WERE DIP SHIT"

His panicked flailing was getting the best of him, he couldn't remember how to put two sheets and a pillowcase together.

"Your mom and dad were slobs, hobos weren't they recruit? You maggot. Didn't they teach you how to make a rack? Get that rack in Marine Corps order NOW. DO YOU UNDERSTAND ME?"

"SIR YES SIR!"

I thought he was going to faint. Back and forth I flew, hollering and badgering, from one end of the squad bay to the other, a hurricane in green with the single-minded intention to destroy the mindset and tranquility that had kept these young men soft.

Some would think everything looked nearly perfect, but a drill instructor will always find something to correct. Even "perfect" can be corrected.

Enjoying the moment

Their former DIs had been removed for some reason. I didn't know why, nor did I care. I just knew they hadn't done their job. They'd left behind a platoon of pansy boy scouts. Two weeks out from graduation, those guys should have been in tip-top platinum shape.

When my Senior Drill Instructor finally showed up, I saw the pleading looks they cast in his direction, but there would be no mercy. He was a tough ol' Marine himself, a square headed unibrowed vet with piercing eyes and a couple of fillings in his teeth that looked like they were made of shell casings. Not the type to coddle.

He told me to exit, his eyes gleaming through the scowl on his swarthy face. He had seen torn-up squad bays before, and, although I might have gone overboard, he had given me a job to do and I had done it; though perhaps over-enthusiastically.

Heading up the catwalk outside, I could still hear the half-hearted "yes sirs" as he ordered them to put back everything I'd just torn apart.

My, my, I thought. That shouldn't have been necessary in third phase, but I had to admit, I did enjoy it.

Little did I know that reports of my first day would spread across Parris Island; rattling the cages of officers whose job it was to safeguard the reputation of the base's training procedures. Even a hint of recruit abuse could bring press hounds in, sniffing at our perimeters, eager to bash our decades of old and proven training traditions. So, call it karma or manifest destiny, discipline was about to grab me by the starched collar.

Yet, for the moment, I was on cloud nine. I had entered the arena with a little trepidation, not really sure how I would come across on deck. I had surprised myself. I can do this job, I thought. With excellence!

Fresh out of training

I had been out of drill instructor training school for a week. My "cover", the traditional, olive drab Smokey-The-Bear drill instructor hat, hadn't even completely settled onto my jar-shaped head. No worries there though. Within just a few weeks the South Carolina summer would melt it around my temples. That first summer would be a real scorcher, one I would never forget.

I slept great the night before my first day on deck; no nerves, no anxiety. I didn't even dream. I had been a Marine long enough that making one should be a walk in the park. I knew how a Marine dressed, smelled, acted, ate, and how they took a dump. All I had to do was keep that image in mind as I stripped a recruit of his flaws and remolded him through demonstration and correction into a proper Marine. Sure, it would require focus and nineteen-hour days on my part, but that was just the grunt side of it, the military reality with which I was already conditioned.

Confidence wasn't a problem. There were no problems!

I had called my wife and gone over the day with her, so at 2300, I turned off the lamp and rolled over into oblivion, one arm clutching the cool side of the white pillow to my face. Like I said, no dreams. Not even the rustle of one.

At 0400 the alarm went off. I scratched the stubble that would soon be razored away, dressed in my PT gear and left - joining the seventy or so other DI graduates for one last morning workout together. The tall harsh lights of the PT blacktop struggled against the muggy darkness, a losing battle that was re-fought every 24 hours. Not until the sun pawed its way over fields and ferns and the ever present swarm of brown moths would the real day begin. Until then, everything was just a warm-up.

It's funny how you grow accustomed to the irritants of routines, and even learn to love them. They are reliable, the mosquitoes, the sand-fleas, the humidity. Even the alligators have their place in your ordered community. You do push-ups while they pad their bellies with the marsh mud, hissing and grunting in the distance behind the steady, authoritative count of your company First Sergeant.

"Fifty more, OOORAAH?" yelled the jarhead next to me, beginning an extra round of push-ups.

"Why not," I grunted, breathing hard under the glorious feel of strain. "Got anything better to do at

0600?" The First Sergeant was a stern man who loved the flex of his own muscles. PT could be a punishing test of endurance, but if he could do it, so could we!

We ended that morning's workout with a three-mile run, our voices cutting the air with a perfect blend of tenor and baritone as blurry streaks of grey light unveiled details of the island's horizon:

> "I wanna be a drill instructor
> I wanna cut off all my hair
> I wanna be a drill instructor
> I wanna wear that Smokey Bear…"

Turned loose

After PT, I returned to my house, an affectionate name for the squad bay where I spent most nights. There I undertook the relieving and refining processes that would qualify me for a day's service. I paused between shaving cream swipes and admired my face in the mirror; it wasn't so much a handsome face – it was an appropriate face. God made my face and the only place it looked good was on a Marine Drill Instructor. I headed for the chow hall and gobbled down breakfast, eager for my first day as "the real thing."

By 0630 or so, all of us graduates had gathered at the squad bay and were chatting and checking each others orders and ribbing the ones that had easy starts. Mine would be one of those, a platoon in their eleventh week. How hard could that be? All they had left was final drill competition and graduation preparation. I recall wondering why they had assigned new leadership so late in the game, but didn't dwell on the irregularity long. Orders are orders. Maybe they were switching things up to keep the recruits on their toes.

We squared away our Charlie's. Then off we marched to our new assignments.

Our platoon halted outside of Charlie Company's headquarters and I was escorted into the building where the First Sergeant's door stood slightly ajar, directly to my left. I knocked and heard a gruff, "Well, get in here!"

Entering, I greeted First Sergeant Cline, the bushy eye-browed and jocular head of First Battalion Charlie Company. He stood to shake my hand. He and I wouldn't become close, but I would retain respect for him.

"Welcome to Charlie Company, Sergeant McDugle," he said. "It's a pleasure to meet you. Your instructors gave you high marks and thought you'd make a fine DI. You'll be working with some great hats (a term used for Drill Instructors) some really fine Marines. In fact, Sergeant Barcon's a legend. He's sharp. If you have any problems whatsoever, go to him first."

"Now, let me tell you how I like to operate. I don't like looking over people's shoulders, so stay on top of things, okay? It'll keep us all out of trouble. Do the paperwork, dot your 'I's, cross your 'T's, and keep me informed. And if you have to put a boot up a recruit's backside don't leave a mark. You understand?" His eyebrows pinched together above his nose. "I've been down that road before and I hate trying to deflect the fallout. Read me?"

"Yes, First Sergeant," I answered.

We talked a few minutes more and then he sent me to the DI house where I met Sergeant Barcon and Sergeant Jabbs. Nice guys, but I wouldn't know them for long.

"Whaddya think?" Sergeant Jabbs asked after we had spent some time getting acquainted. "Feel ready to open the gates of hell on these recruits?"

"Sure," I answered without hesitation. Was I insecure? No. Curious as to how I would be received? Yes. Jittery? No. "Just make constant corrections, right?"

"Yup. You know the routine! Shake 'em up a bit."

"Absolutely," I said, sucking down the last of my coffee through a smile. "Absolutely…"

McDugle on Deck

The platoon had already had their midday chow when I entered their squad bay. I glanced starboard at my reflection in the nearest porthole as I walked on deck; noting that I looked razor sharp and on-point. For those of you non-military types a porthole is a window and starboard is to the right. I strolled onto the barrack floor, which I used to reassure myself of my presentation. The Marine Corps is a department of the Navy, the men's department, as I like to make sure they know and understand. As a part of the Navy, most terms are ship-referenced.

I stopped and stared down the aisle. The recruits were clumped in little green groups, or most of them, at least—laughing and jabbering about who knows what - with their boots un-bloused and their skivvy shirts un-tucked. A few were sitting on their racks. The squad bay looked a mess, especially for third phase recruits. The first recruit that laid eyeballs on me yelled "Drill Instructor on Deck". Their "snap-to" was not quick or sharp, are these recruits really in third phase?

Who did these guys think they were? This was third phase, two weeks from graduation! They hadn't even heard the hatch shut. That's when Recruit Anderson sauntered up.

"Yo, sir…can I tell you a joke?"

I've already described what happened next; a hurricane made landfall and left indescribable carnage. Recruits were left wobbly, wet, and near weeping.

Reflecting on the scenario at chow that evening, I wondered, how on earth did those guys get this far in training? The other drill instructors at chow had enjoyed a great first day and were sharing humorous anecdotes about their new recruits. Wide-eyed kids straight off the bus. Some recruits were from Redneck Corner, Fifth and Broadway, small-town USA, or wherever. All fresh starts that had gone by the book, lucky guys.

I slid my chow tray onto a stack of dirty ones and headed back to the squad-bay. Running into some buddies, I grumbled about the platoon of pansy misfit pukes I'd inherited and how I'd turned their world upside down and thrashed 'em good. They all agreed that's what they would've done too, not normally a third phase event. "You did the right thing, McDugle, so don't sweat it. They'll be better Marines for it in the end.

"Yeah, but is it too late?" I wondered. "They've got ten weeks of bad habits that need to be unlearned and there's only two weeks left in their cycle."

"That is a sad, sad situation," one of my buddies said. "Somebody did them a great disservice by being so lax with them. It could cost them their lives on a battlefield."

I remember my best friend telling me years ago that everyone has the ability to change their direction but I wondered if it was too late for these recruits.

The discussion went on for a while as we debated whether or not it was possible to turn those rouges into tight Marines in the short amount of time remaining. I didn't think it could be done. Most of the other hats didn't either, but suggested I make their last two weeks harder than the previous eleven combined.

I had already made up my mind to do just that. I would give them a taste of McDugle's private little hell. I hit the rack that night at peace with the challenge ahead of me—anticipating it, really—and slept like a Marine should always sleep, sufficiently, but lightly with one eye open.

Facing the music

There's nothing like stepping out at 0500 into the epic, movie-like atmosphere of Parris Island base. The steady clomp-clomp-clomp of marching and the staccato drone of cadence are its heartbeat and a Marine is just one tiny green blood cell in the vastness of its sublime organization. Or, depending on one's view, of it's punishing but splendid predictability.

After chow, I headed for the DI house. As I approached, I could hear a conversation taking place behind the hatch, a very animated one by the sound of it. But when I stepped inside, things suddenly got awfully quiet. Barcon and Jabbs glanced at each other.

"McDugle, the Colonel wants to see you right away. I don't know much about it, but apparently the recruits made some allegations that found their way up the chain." Sergeant Barcon scratched his grape and glanced away. "Fuckin' pussy platoon."

"Whadja do?" Sergeant Jabbs chuckled. "Make 'em piss and drink it?"

"Heh-heh, no," I said. "I went off on the recruits a little, but nobody croaked. A few had to swim in their own puddles though. So, who filed the report?"

"I don't know and it doesn't matter," Barcon said, "but lemme give you some advice." He leaned forward and stared at me intensely, like a beefy, enwisened goblin. "Don't deny nothin' if you did it, and don't admit to something if you didn't. Stand your ground. Hell, you have been here less than 24 hours and the Colonel will take that into consideration. But, see, he's not around these recruits on a daily basis and he doesn't know what a bunch of piss-ant mama boy pukes that platoon is. Plus...he's gotta deal with public relations. I'll stand up for ya though...I think you did great for your first day."

He winked at the Jabbs. "Tore into 'em and got their attention, what the hell is wrong with that?"

"Alright," I said, "I'll go face the music. I'll let you know how it turns out."

I made my way to the Colonel's office in stony silence. I respected rank highly, but wasn't afraid of it, so I kept my bearing as the morning sun spilled out of a cloud bank onto the blue-grey roof of the 1st Battalion Headquarters. I knew that justice and integrity were Marines' chalices and I had earned the right to drink from them whereas the recruits were still just civilians who'd been, well…exercised a lot.

Up the broad steps I went and through the mahogany hatch, past the garrison flags with brass capping and walls of photos that celebrated current and past leadership. Hallways branched off before me, tunnels that surrounded my footsteps with a disconcerting echo. I felt like a boy on his way to the principal's office.

A corporal at a counter asked my name, then rang the Colonel. I was waved past and entered the Colonel's office, shutting the hatch behind me. Centering myself on his desk, I said "Sir, Sergeant McDugle, reporting as ordered, Sir!" I stood at attention, waiting for him to say, "At ease."

I did not get an "at ease."

"Sergeant McDugle," he growled, leaning forward over his desk ready to pounce, "I would kick your fucking ass out of the corps if you hadn't been here less than 24 hours."

He wasn't wasting any time.

The colonel's presence, like any veteran officer's, was not a veneered contrivance; he had authority and knew it. He was not a chiseled colonel but one that probably came up through administrative ranks – definitely not a grunt. Surely he would take the word of a three time combat vet over the word of some pussy recruit.

At the moment, he was an angry man, with a red, puffy face and a twitch. I confess to becoming irritated as he began to bawl me out, informing me that I had been charged with forty-eight counts of physical abuse and thirty-eight counts of verbal abuse. Didn't the fact that I was a combat veteran count for something? I felt like it would have been courteous to hear my side of the story before jumping to conclusions.

"This is no game, Sergeant," he continued, ruffling through a stack of papers. "See these? These reports are headed other places, and I'm not sure I can stop them. One of the recruit's mothers happens to be an attorney, and she could bring us into court if she had a mind to. These allegations have the potential to blemish your record, and more importantly, the character of the Corps, and that infuriates the hell out of me. Now, you know the rules, Sergeant McDugle, so tell me what on earth got into that thick fucking grape of yours and made you think it was okay to lay hands on these boys?"

"Sir," I began, realizing the Colonel had already come to his own conclusions and that what I said would not matter, "the incident wasn't as extreme as all that. I had just walked into the squad bay when a dark green recruit approached me and asked if I wanted to hear a joke. He didn't request permission to speak and his appearance for a third phase recruit was shit, so I commenced to do what Drill Instructors do and reminded him of where he is. I then proceeded to execute incentive training on both him and the rest of his nasty platoon. Sir, I never touched a recruit. I wouldn't do that on my first day. And their claims of verbal abuse are exaggerated. I was loud and threatened them but I never used half the obscenities indicated in those reports. In my opinion, these recruits are an absolute mess and the whole fucking lot of them should be sent back to first phase!"

The Colonel leaned forward once again in his chair and railed at me for fifteen more minutes. I couldn't believe it. I had been a Marine for six years, three combat tours and had even helped to train our foreign allies, so it ticked me off that he was taking the word of some coward nasty fucking recruits over a veteran Marine.

I understood the seriousness of the situation. The Marine Corps has a reputation and the delicacy of the situation required everybody to dance around each other's words and threats a bit. I learned perception is reality.

In the end, I was sent to S3 (a maintenance unit) for thirty days where I was supposed to mow lawns and pick up trash. After that, I would be assigned to a new batch of pukes, fresh off the bus, so I could take a whole cycle through from the beginning. Whew, I thought. That was a close one. I had to think about what was more important, my career or training these boys so they would survive in combat… My career was not nearly as important.

S3

S3 wasn't so bad, I had been on battlefields, after all, and survived them. Plus, I knew I hadn't done anything seriously wrong; I had just scared some kids that hadn't been expecting it, nothing more than that, so my conscience was clear.

I had to let it go. In S3, there was a sergeant who had been a drill instructor, who listened to my story and determined he wasn't going to have me mowing lawns. He had plenty of young Marines who could square away the lawn, so I hung out for a month, worked out twice a day and helped the sergeant as much as I could. My pay had been suspended for the thirty days and I was banned from associating with anyone in Charlie Company, DIs included, so I was antsy and bored as hell. I was also instructed not to interact with recruits and to avoid their chow hall and barracks. No problem. The time went by quickly.

Since then, I have never had a complaint—not one. In fact, thanks to the mentorship of more seasoned DI's, I became a trusted Marine drill instructor, who was able to produce others like myself, while keeping the respect of the other hats around me. Did I soften up? Nope. I became tougher actually, and wiser as I learned to refine and balance procedure with intimidation.

The platoon I'd "terrorized" graduated midway through my exile, but the kids who filed the charges were ordered back a cycle and had to repeat a portion of their training. I hope to hell they got good training, their lives and the lives of others are on the line.

Eventually, I was returned to Charlie Company, where I joined a group of DIs picking up a new batch of recruits. They were delighted to have me on board and told me that my reputation had spread among the DI ranks, eliciting an admiration I hadn't expected. They knew I could hold my own and handle whatever the recruits threw at me. The admin officers weren't so thrilled, however. Their job is to maintain order and make sure the operation continues to run smooth without sending someone to the brig. I know they thought I was a loose cannon but eventually the memory of the incident dimmed, to both their relief and mine.

Meanwhile, I came to love the crusty, experienced drill instructors that took me under their wings. I had penetrated their inner circle in one fell swoop, without even trying, while my fellow DI graduates were held at arm's distance by these surly veterans who valued trust and loyalty as earned commodities. They taught me the importance of winning the loyalty of recruits, a time-consuming process that has no shortcuts. You have to stay on them night and day; you have to live with them, march with them, eat with them, endure the heat with them and constantly correct them. You don't just dish-out hardships; you set the example and live hardships with them. A drill instructor is a recruit's only constant, a dependable, if fearful beacon in their tear and sweat blurred world.

They also taught me about the "invisible line."

You see, Marine training procedures are extremely well defined on paper and fixed in their allowances of what one can and can't do regarding discipline.

But, for all the rigidity, there are lines that can be crossed. It's all a matter of viewpoint. Within the inner circle of DI brotherhood, most restrictions are seen as an expandable perimeter, like the flexible sides of a balloon. There is some give to it. In fact it has to give in order to train Marines.

It's imperative that a recruit's paradigm is defined by an understanding of this. He must realize that he can never relax. Sometimes they arrive with certain fixed notions; a drill instructor can't hit me (do not push one too far) and a drill instructor can't cuss at me or call me other names. A recruit with that mentality will quickly learn that a drill instructor lives in a balloon, not a box, and he'll gladly show you how far he can stretch it, and not just because he can. The truth is, he cares more about preparing Marines for combat survival than following rules and ending up with boy scouts that could get themselves or others killed in action.

Someone who joins the Marine Corps thinking, "I'll let them push me this far, but no farther," is going to be un-trainable. They have to believe—know—that a drill instructor's response to any situation or attitude anytime can't be predicted. If he threatens to stick copperhead teeth under your fingernails, you'd better believe he might!

And anyway, there's always the butt stroke of a rifle or a quick punch to the gut - many a tough guy has had his clock cleaned by a drill instructor fed up with stupidity. A drill instructor has a lot of resources at his disposal.

Most of the DIs I knew walked the line pretty well. They were willing to take risks, push the envelope, and put their rank and career on the line to make sure the pukes they were training could survive in combat. Mean-tempered Marines wouldn't make it into the drill instructor training program - the selection process is so rigorous. Occasionally, I ran across a few who were jaded or just plain tired, but they were rare and were weeded out pretty quickly.

The good ones make becoming a Marine a very difficult thing, which makes a Marine a rarity and of great value to our nation.

As for me, I couldn't wait to start with a fresh platoon. I had gotten off to a rocky start and had to take some lumps, but it had only served to wet my appetite.

Yep, I thought, while ironing my starched uniform…I'm gonna like this.

Becoming SGT Death, Island terror

I didn't find out until years later that I was known as Sergeant Death among some recruits. Some of my cohorts were known as Sergeant Destruction and Sergeant Satan. Nicknames like these are whispered from bunk to bunk during the wee hours of the night, so we never knew of our hefty monikers.

They are funny, but not important. As a DI, your sole and complete focus is training, not earning titles or ribbons.

Recruits show up in buses and are processed through a receiving company before being turned over to their drill instructors. Often, drill instructors take time between training cycles to process DIs, screaming at the recruits as they exited the transport buses, eyes as big as Carolina moons.

Most poolies were in poor shape. And there were always a few who were underweight and a few who were well overweight. To me they all looked sloppy and unqualified—scared kids clinging to their former tough guy identities as though they'd sold their souls to the devil.

The devil wasn't involved, but they had certainly sold their souls.

In June of 1994, I finished my time at S3 and was ready to move on. I was assigned to a fresh platoon in Charlie Company and waited eagerly alongside the other hats for the processing DIs to bring them to the squad bay. It was as sterile as a hospital there. You couldn't find a speck of dust if you tried and the recruits would learn to keep it this way.

Shortly after they marched in, to their dismay, they were commanded to sit asshole to belly button, with their legs spread and their crotches jammed into the backside of the man in front of them. The short recruits were up front and the tall ones in the back.

Then the Company Commander introduced the Series Commander, one of the tallest Marines I've ever seen, who then introduced the Series Gunnery Sergeant who in turn introduced the Senior DI.

The Senior DI gave his SDI speech which includes letting the recruits know that discipline and spirit are hallmarks of marine training and a marine never lies, cheats or compromises, and a marine never steals. The senior let the recruits know that the drill instructors would not give up on them even when many of them would give up on themselves. "We will treat you as we do our fellow marines with firmness, fairness, dignity and compassion." The senior would then introduce the other drill instructors.

The recruits were officially ours now. We began to instruct the recruits in the correct way to stand at attention. Drill Instructor Sergeant Flannery, who would become a good friend of mine, began his first period of instruction while I grabbed a footlocker and stood at attention on top of it demonstrating the proper form as he began his cacophonous oration:

"Sit up straight and get your eyeballs on me. I SAID SIT UP STRAIGHT AND GET YOUR EYEBALLS ON ME! Notice how the drill instructors feet are at a 45-degree angle. His heels are on line and touching. His legs are straight but not stiff at the knees. His hips and shoulders are level and his arms hang naturally to the side. His fingers are in a natural curl and his thumb is along the trouser seam. His chest is lifted and his chin is tucked in slightly.

Notice when I walk in front of the drill instructor his head and eyes remain to the front, but most importantly his mouth is shut. I say again, his mouth is shut.

While aboard Marine Corps Recruit Depot Parris Island, South Carolina, you will address all personnel, Navy, Marines, and Civilians at the position of attention."

This instruction was broadcasted quite loudly with spit flying. Immediately following, our senior Drill Instructor, Staff Sergeant Martin informed the recruits that he was about to give them a command. His eyes narrowed on them. "And when I do, I want you to find the footlocker with your name on it and come to the position of attention on the line in front of it. And you better move, Recruits! Do you understand me?" "Sir Yes sir" "I said DO YOU UNDERSTAND ME?" "SIR YES SIR"

He hesitated and glared at them, then barked his order.

All hell broke loose.

As they scrambled to locate their footlockers, we lit into them like screaming banshees, dodging back and forth from one to the other, hollering at the top of our lungs: "GET ON LINE, YOU SORRY EXCUSE FOR A PIG! Hurry up! I said HURRY! What is taking you so long you fucking maggots? What the hell? You can't even find your name in alphabetical order? You remember your name, don't you? GET THE FUCK ON LINE NOW!" A drill instructors voice is hard to understand as they speak fast and constantly bark orders.

It wasn't uncommon for a recruit's bladder to let loose during this initial exposure to their new daddies. I've witnessed it on many occasions: the darkening of a trouser crotch and the uncomfortable hydration of new socks with a puddle on the deck. As a matter of fact, my record is six grown men pissing in one day, a testimony to the effectiveness of volume and intimidation. I can't deny I find it humorous. The chaos serves a very important purpose in that over time it conditions the recruits to carry out orders under duress, a critical battlefield virtue. The fact is I enjoy yelling so loud blood flies out of my throat, and the pleasure of screwing my face into various contortions. It helps to make a tough job more stimulating.

Tommy Hamilton, a recruit of mine from a later cycle, describes this first period of instruction from his point of view:

"We were taken to the squad bay where Staff Sergeant Thomas had us sit down Indian-style up front by the quarter deck. Captain Stoppa came out and talked to us, then introduced us to the drill instructors responsible for our training, Senior Drill Instructor Staff Sergeant Wooten, EDI Sergeant Schaeffer, and Drill Instructor Sergeant McDugle. Staff Sergeant Wooten gave his SDI speech, and then turned us over to Sergeant McDugle. Sergeant McDugle had these scary, piercing, light blue eyes; imagine a drill instructor in your mind and he's exactly what you'd get. Drill Instructor Sergeant

McDugle had Sergeant Schaeffer stand on a footlocker then described at the top of his lungs how to stand at attention properly while Sergeant Schaeffer demonstrated it. We were informed that this was the only way we would address any Marine, sailor, or civilian while on Parris Island."

After the chaos, when they'd all found their places and locked up their money valuable bags, we marched them to the chow hall. I remember thinking these guys are the most uncoordinated blockheads I've ever seen. Was I this slow and stupid when I was a recruit?

Before allowing them to file into the chow hall, I warned them that if I heard a peep out of anyone they would all suffer the consequences. There would be no mercy. They were also instructed concerning social graces:

"Ears" "open sir" "I said EARS" "OPEN SIR" "You will sit at your table with your heels together, your left hand resting palm-down on your left knee, while you convey the allotted nutrition from your plate to your mouth with smooth, steady motion," I said. "And if I hear one word—one 'pass the salt'—you can kiss your potatoes goodbye. Finished or not we're outta here!" By the look in their eyes, I could tell they perceived this wasn't going to go well for them. They scuttled in, hungry but edgy, and formed a long, green line, without as much as a cough. Silverware rattled and trays clanked but other than that you could've heard a pin drop.

After the last recruit had been served, Sergeant Flannery and I, without having chow ourselves, proceeded to initiate another lesson in discipline. SGT Flannery said "Get these sorry excuses for humans out of the chow hall". The recruits had only been seated for a few minutes.

"You miserable dimwits," I shouted, stomping up the center aisle between the long tables with a finger pointing toward the exit. "Get up and out, RIGHT NOW! I heard that whisper! You maggots cannot even obey the simplest of instructions, GET OUT OF MY CHOW HALL RIGHT NOW!"

Had we heard anything? No. But out of ninety recruits, chances were somebody had said something to somebody else. It was a devious head-game, but it planted the idea of corporate responsibility in a grand, unforgettable sweep. Mess with a man's food, sleep or money and you'll get his attention! We repeated the scenario (with subtle variations) for four or five more meals and then let them settle into regular eating rituals.

Out the hatch they scrambled into the afternoon sun, and sure enough, I overheard one frustrated recruit chastise another as he elbowed him in the ribs, "I told you not to say anything, you puss." The face of the guilty party reddened as he realized he'd been exposed. He would take some heat for it later, but oh well—lesson learned. When a Drill Instructor says to keep your mouth shut, he means it!

Squinting in the bright yellow glare, I ordered them to come to the position of attention. Sergeant Flannery was staring at the ground, concealing a mild smile and shaking his head. I could read his mind: what a bunch of uncoordinated double left footed peons.. They're about as graceful as a three-legged dog tripping over each other's bootlaces. But eventually I had some type of platoon formation standing before me.

"Knowledge recruit get out your BIBLE." I commanded.

Marine recruits have no down time, if they are waiting for anything they are kept busy. They are not allowed to "turn off" until they hit the rack. And the Marine Corps bible, or "book of knowledge" is the primary tool used to keep their minds focused on Marine knowledge at all times.

"Since you don't know how to keep your pie-holes shut, knowledge will have to suffice for both your meal and your dessert," I yelled, "which should be more than sufficient fuel for your lazy asses, because knowledge is power. Beginning right now, right this very second, you will learn to eagerly love and devour every consonant, vowel,

Who is this guy?

The following weeks flew by, for me at least. For the recruits, I am sure time went by at an agonizing crawl. Marine boot camp is made up of three phases, each lasting approximately four weeks, which are set by command.

Phase One consists of getting the recruits into shape physically, which means lots of PT (Physical Training). As they progress, they become stronger and more demands are put on them. They will experience more rounds of "thrashing," "quarter decking," or "I.T." which are various Marine terms for Incentive Training—punishments dished out for even the most minute infractions. They will learn to march, to take orders and in the last week of the phase to survive in the water.

In Phase Two, they learn Marksmanship and experience a field-week and a team-week. In Phase Three, they'll be put into realistic combat situations and undergo warrior training, including hand-to-hand combat. Nowadays, the Crucible tops off the phase, followed by graduation and all its preparations. The Corps hadn't yet developed the Crucible in the early nineties when I was a DI.

I developed my own phases as well. I learned that steadily mounting degrees of intensity increased the impact of training on a recruit.

For instance, as I've previously stated, you can't hit a recruit - you can't get caught hitting a recruit. During the first couple of weeks, they shouldn't even be pushed around. The yelling is enough. Even the gang members, though familiar with some level of violence, haven't been treated disrespectfully. So it's a shocker when you are all alone to be incessantly stripped down with words.

They get used to it quicker than you'd imagine. They start thinking I can handle this.

When I sensed immunity forming, I'd raise the stress level by getting personal with them and mix name-calling into my cussing. I might even mention a mother's name or the name of a girl friend from back home. That woke 'em up. What did he just call me? How the hell does he know my girlfriend?

One particular tough guy thought he had me all figured out. He would stare past me as though I was nothing but a sputtering volcano. He was a Florida beach bum and the toughest thing he had probably ever experienced was a high school football game. I had a new play for him though. Since the recruit loved the beach and the water I thought I would make him feel right at home. First we started with a trashcan full of water in the middle of the squad bay, which I kicked over with my boot. The water ran across the smooth glass like cement on the deck. I had the recruit pick a playmate for the beach and the two of them with towel in hand would race from one end of the squad bay to the next, towel on the floor, two hands on the towel and two legs pushing as fast as they could to soak up the water and wrench it back in the trashcan. The slowest recruit would then go visit the sandy beach outside called the PIT. The first two laps of this exercise seemed fun - until they realized every drop of water from that trashcan had better be returned. I don't have to tell you this but as they were soaking up the water sweat was drenching the topside of the towel. "Every drop on my deck will be dried up, welcome to the Beach Boys concert of 1993, Do you enjoy the beach recruits?"

There was a pause, you could tell they were weighing the tricks of my question and then…"Sir, no sir. These recruits don't like the beach sir!"

"How dare you, you nasty 'sack religious' puke! Do you mean to tell me you think God did a poor job of creating the beach? You don't like God's creativity! You will learn to love the beach do you understand me!! "Sir, YES sir"

"Recruit, **you** have ten seconds to get in my pit and demonstrate to me the joys of building castles and throwing sand up to God on the beach and the whole time you will be apologizing to God for your lack of understanding and appreciating His creation! DO YOU HEAR ME?"

"Sir, yes sir!"

Outside, the afternoon clouds were gathering to pour a South Carolina weather cocktail on us, but we had enough time for Recruit Mason to show appreciation for the beach. I made the whole platoon participate, of course, to their chagrin. The Marine Corp is not about soloing.

Meanwhile, the other drill instructors slipped away and gathered all the sheets and pillowcases in the squad bay and made a tight, giant knot out of them.

After the demonstration and a few hundred pushups, I let the recruits fall back in. Panting heavily through tightly closed lips, sand covering every cell on their bodies, if they could dare eye me it would be with a new found tremor.

Who is this guy?

As time went on, if getting physical was required, I would certainly resort to it. A twist to the side-meat, a rifle butt to the chest, a finger to a pressure point—all of these recaptured a recruit's attention and emphasized the perception that a drill instructor has no law.

Fifty percent of my recruits never needed to be roughed up. For most of them, regular visits to The Pit were sufficient. Some on the other hand needed to know that I would pull out their juggler and shove it up their ass if they needed it.

Close call

July rolled around and under its blazing sun I found that I was learning too, and at a rapid pace. There is a weave that joins but separates officers from enlisted staff like myself, and we all learn the dodges and interactions of its requirements. It demands that we give respect but it also demands that we give room, and therein is the delicate balance of the military tapestry.

I recall one time when enthusiasm got the better of me and I tipped slightly out of that honored balance, which was permissible as long as no one was watching.

I was up on a recruit, right in his face, spitting fire at him, and had gotten a hold of him by his throat. Lightly, mind you, with a bit of a white knuckle squeeze, I wanted to fucking kill him. He'd said something smart when he thought I wasn't around, but I'd heard his whole whiny tirade.

Suddenly, out of the corner of my eye, I caught the shine of polished brass. A Captain was passing by one of the portholes and had glanced in. Quickly, I stepped back to an arm's distance and continued to reprimand the recruit, keeping my flow, but chiding myself on the inside. I knew the perception of what I had done and knew that it couldn't have looked good.

Well, thankfully that Captain, a grunt, understood "the weave" and gave me room. He pulled me aside afterwards, away from the recruits, and with all the grace and tact of a seasoned infantry officer, gave me some of the best advice I ever received as a drill instructor.

"Perception," he told me, "is nine-tenths of the law. If you're perceived to be beating up a recruit, then you are beating up a recruit. Adopt that as a guideline and it will benefit not only the recruits, but it will benefit you and your career as a drill instructor as well."

That Captain was a mustang, an officer that came from enlisted ranks, so he understood my job, gave me the length of line to do it according to the way I saw fit, and blessed me with a precept that kept me from ever again straining past the taut point of any situation.

God bless the wise Marine officers who view the whole, and aren't narrowly focused on their tiny corner of authority and dominion. I encountered many who understood what it takes to make Marines and they covered my backside more than once. Others were pencil pushers who knew rules but not the effect the rules had on making marines.

My way or the highway

My voice changed through that first cycle too. I'd never had a problem being heard. I've always been loud, but my tone was beginning to alter. What had at first been a buttery belt was becoming a gravel-coated roar that would rival a rock singer for edge.

Think about it. You're up at 0400 after maybe five hours of sleep and hollering from reveille until the sun goes down, and more often than not, long after that. Your vocal chords get fried. Your pitch deepens and eventually you are the proud dispatcher of what has been fondly dubbed "the frog voice"—a drill instructor's number one weapon. My best friend could speak things into existence. He would tell me that if you say things out loud that don't exist today, but you want them to, the speaking out loud allows it to sink into your brain and you begin to believe you can and will achieve it.

The "Frog Voice" is unique to each man and it is not a contrivance—it is a physical adaptation. Its development begins at drill instructor school, while repeating cadence—belting from the belly because you can't breathe and run at the same time any other way.

But the grit and gravel becomes more defined as the drill instructor matures. Mine, I am proud to say, has a particularly threatening crunch to it.

I also began to look the part. Not that I didn't before, but as I evolved, my character and expressions became more fixed—I didn't have to put on and take off a "look" anymore. I was no longer playing the part of a DI, I was a DI. Routine was molding me even as it molded the recruits. In time, like many drill instructors before me, I became a drill instructor's drill instructor, a poster-boy for the title. I'd had the raw ugly look to begin with, given by God at birth, and combat and the position weathered me with its finishing touches.

It suited me just fine.

It was nearly the end of Phase One and time for the Confidence Course, a staple of boot camp training in all branches of the armed forces.

Marching the platoon to chow the night before, I recalled my own boot camp experience with the course eight years earlier. I had been nervous, unsure whether or not I would complete all of its challenges successfully. I had not been a gifted athlete as a teenager and was plagued by insecurities and self-doubts, but in the end, I made good marks on the course and my confidence level had been boosted. I hoped the same for this batch of maggots.

As they filed down the chow line, Sergeant Flannery and I took our places at the opposite end. By now, the "fat bodies", the overweight recruits whose uniforms were marked with painted stripes so the world would know they were fat, knew we'd be waiting for them. One by one they lined up in front of us until six or eight of them stood there, trays outstretched. Fat bodies eat last - they knew. Their rations were cut to a precisely determined dietary restriction and this was our "double-check". No extra potatoes, no breads, no cake. They were starting to look pretty fit. In a few more weeks, they'd be virtually indistinguishable from the other recruits—strong and polished!

Sergeant Flannery flicked some gravy off one recruit's mashed potato pile. As it splashed on his eyebrows, he grimaced at his girth. "There. You can go sit down now, but don't lemme catch you eating one bite of potatoes and you had better eat all of your green beans. If I see even a pinch of potatoes missing, I'll take you to the pit and work it back outta you before it has time to reach your gut. Do you understand me?"

"Sir, yes SIR!"

He hustled away, dismayed, but eager to gobble down what he had.

"Now who we gonna blame this on?" I asked.

He grinned. "The new line guy over there dishing out potatoes to the fat bodies."

"Never miss a thing, do ya?"

"Nope!" Off he went, bellowing.

The anorexic guys weren't off the hook either. They were double rationed and they were the first to go through as they had double the meal to eat. After the meal they'd line up and we'd make sure their trays were spotless. I have made more than a few suck up the last dribbles of their corn juice.

After the mob had eaten, we ran them to the squad bay. We could sense their restless energy—they were excited about the Confidence Course. It would be a nice break from the routines of marching and classes and incentive training.

Drill instructors look forward to the Confidence Course too. It's really our first glimpse at the results of our work. Many of these knuckle heads couldn't do a hundred pushups when they joined, but tomorrow they'd climb higher, run faster, and conquer more fears than they'd ever imagined. The Marine Corp is a mental game. We might lose a few, who'd be sent to a new platoon to start from the beginning, but not many. And after the day's harrowing challenges, we would seldom see the civilian in these recruits rear its ugly head again.

At around 1900 Sergeant Flannery took off for the day. I informed the recruits that after cleaning and securing their weapons, they could shower and then I'd give them an hour of square away time. In their square away time they could write letters, polish boots, iron uniforms, etc. But they had to do these things my way using the particular methods I had taught them. I never left them to themselves.

"Remember how to write your letters, Recruit Morgan? You sit on the end of your footlocker with your back straight and your heels together, feet at a 45 degree angle, your back is straight and your mouth is shut. And don't purse your lips while you're thinking what to say..."

"Sir, yes SIR!"

Finally, it was 2045. I rubbed at the day's sweat that had thickened on the back of my neck and hollered down the bay, "Health and hygiene inspection... move!" They knew the drill: underwear only, and they'd be showered. I stood in front of the first, Recruit Adams.

He was smart, and had been a decent high school athlete, but I could tell he had to bite his Boston tongue all the time, so I'd push his buttons for fun occasionally. He was a quick learner though, and wore the red badge of sand flea bites on his legs with determined stoicism. Others wore them all the way up to their waists, but the light bulbs hadn't come on yet. More about those guys later.

"Report!"

His response was instant and precisely articulated.

"Sir, this recruit has no personal, medical, or physical problems to report at this time, SIR!" He turned his head from side to side and flipped out his hands, showing me the backs and fronts as he spun slowly around. I made sure there were no cuts, bruises, or abrasions that he'd not reported and that he'd showered and trimmed his ear hairs and nose hairs. And that he smelled the way he **ought** to smell—like Listerine and Aqua Velva. Exactly like the Marine right next to him.

I repeated the process down the squad bay. It wasn't unusual for an injury to go unreported. Nobody wanted to cycle over again or appear like a bawl-baby. But training hard with injuries could exacerbate a pre-existing condition so Command insisted we be thorough in our nightly examinations. Most of the dreaded paperwork had to do with detailed notations about a recruit's status derived from these inspections.

Next I ordered them to open their footlockers and stand in front of them with their right arm stretched out so I could see their "money valuable bag." Thirty or so white socks dangled before me, lumpy with wallets, change, and odds and ends.

"Count OFF!" I commanded.

"One," shouted Recruit Adams, and off shot the rest in successive bursts like rounds from an M40. As each declared his number, he tossed his money valuable bag in his footlocker and snapped to the position of attention. This taught them that the Corps was responsible for them and could be trusted. As their drill instructor, I was accountable for every aspect of their lives, including their money valuable bag and the security of their lives - down to the minute detail. Their totality was safe with the Corps and with each other.

I remained with the recruits until lights-out (around 2130) and then stared gloomily at the paperwork I dreaded until 2300. Then I took off, leaving the bulk of it for the night-duty DI, who growled at me about it the next day.

Last Check

After the lights were out, I made my way through the squad bay, making sure the recruits were all in the required sleeping position: fully dressed and at the position of attention, arms at their sides and heels together—on top of their blankets. If I could've made them sleep with one eye open, I would have.

This was not a standard drill instructor procedure—it came from my own manual. Eternal readiness was essential as far as I was concerned and sleeping at attention was one of the "McDugleisms" I employed to help me fulfill that conviction.

When it was my turn for night duty, I would go through the bay every hour or so, waking them up and repositioning them if they'd so much as twitched. A hard flick on the ear would yank them right out of their dreams. They hadn't requested permission to dream anyway. I might quarter deck them, or flip them out of their rack if they did not correct their sleeping position properly.

Tonight I was off, but that still wasn't good news for the recruits because Sergeant Flannery was even meaner than I was. I was sure he had something cunning up his sleeve; after all he was SGT Satan.

I hustled out the absolutely necessary paperwork, the stuff I couldn't leave for someone else then went home for some sound sleep. I kissed my wife on the forehead and listened to the frogs through the vented window of the mobile home we had purchase in the middle of the island.

Sleep came quick.

A McDugle Start

Coffee in hand at 0430, I stepped gingerly down the wooden trailer stairs thinking I need to replace that board before someone falls through it. The coastal air salted everything through, so thin coats of paint became brittle quickly, and everything beneath rusted or rotted.

My uniform creases cut the air as I moved. They would remain stiff regardless of the day. You know your business and I know mine, and part of mine was to make recruits believe that a DI is super-human—a starch stiff and scotch guarded immortal who can wade out of a muddy creek and still look ready for a Colonel's inspection.

After checking in with the others in the DI house, I tiptoed to the squad bay's "whiskey locker." Every squad bay's got one—a storage room filled with toilet-paper rolls, towels, hygiene items, and cleaning supplies. As the recruits finished their shit, shower and shave, I grabbed two huge spray bottles, one filled with Listerine and the other with Aqua Velva after-shave, and hollered for them to get in line and prepare for inspection.

One by one, I blasted them with my sprayers. A few of my shots were good and the Listerine ended up in mouths and Aqua Velva on necks. Some were fidgety however, and it ended up the other way around. That's my story and I'm sticking to it.

Now we were off to a "McDugle" start!

On any other day, we might have had a cleaning session after chow. The recruits would be sent scrambling back and forth picking up ghost turds and scrubbing at nooks and crannies that a toothpick couldn't penetrate. Then we would dump trashcans of water onto the squad bay deck and have them sopping and mopping until the floor shown like a Major's insignia.

But today was going to be hectic enough as it was, I finished my inspection, making sure every weapon was hanging properly on each rack, its safety on and the cable running through its ejection port, locking it securely into place. All their combination locks were set to zero and everything looked uniform and in order, so I got them dressed and marched them to chow,

The normal drill is skinnies first then the regulars, with the fat-bodies pausing to be checked. We gave them five minutes to eat then rushed them outside for 30 minutes of knowledge and some warm-up PT.

> "Momma and Papa were lying in bed
> Momma rolled over, this is what she said:
> A give me some PT!

Good for you
Good for me!"

We formed up, did a quick right face forward march and route step to the Confidence Course.

For a drill instructor, Confidence Course day is filled with stress and hilarious situations. It is hilarious watching a recruit thirty feet in the air holding onto a one inch line as if he was going to die. Those days in particular we have to do more yelling and pushing, than we normally would. In fact, it's non-stop. There's one major difference though, on the CC our cussing and threats are laced with hidden encouragement. The typical recruit mentality as they approach each obstacle is, I have a choice—complete this or deal with the DI behind me, blocking my escape. And despite our scowls, we DIs are rooting for their success. There is no joy in watching someone fail, even if you expected them to. There is a tremendous satisfaction in watching the small grow large, and the large grow larger, on the inside.

This is the main goal of the CC.

Personally, I loved the creativity of the challenges.

The "Confidence Climb" is a particularly difficult one. Recruits have to mount and then leap from one vertical log to the next, each higher than the last. No ropes, no nets. It is like a vertical railroad track put together with telephone poles.

Another is a rope challenge, which consists of swinging across a fairly substantial gap filled with water.

One of the most ominous and foreboding is the "Slide for Life," where three cables stretch off a tower, over a swimming pool and onto the ground. Recruits start by inching along on top of the cable. Once the recruit gets about a third of the way down the cable a Drill Instructor orders him off the top of the cable where he would hang by his hands. From there the recruit has to kick his legs up on top of the cable and inch his way to the ground.

There were other platoons on the course that day, so the atmosphere was a roar of barking DIs and stammering hesitant recruits. I watched with a grin as a stocky DI threatened to make a recruit take a swan dive off the Confidence Climb otherwise known as the Stairway to Heaven if he didn't reach the top rung. Behind me, four DIs had a young Asian recruit surrounded and were using their bodies to block his retreat from the "A-Frame."

The "A-Frame" is a recruit's first real heights challenge. The first tier, reached by a rope climb of about 20 feet takes them through three large logs.

Then they must walk 20 feet over wooden beams to two A-shaped structures that rise another 15 feet in the air. Recruits must climb to the top, swing onto a rope and inch down to the ground. Any fear of heights will reveal itself at this juncture of the course. It was common for recruits to freeze on the first tier but seldom were we unable to coax them through. Rarely—very rarely—a recruit would resist beyond our abilities to persuade and he'd be sent straight to the pit for a little attitude adjustment. The obstacle must be completed to move forward in training.

After the Asian kid got through, I grabbed one of my own nasty larvae by the shoulders and launched him toward the obstacle.

"Line up behind Recruit Waynes," I barked at the rest of my group. "By the book, this obstacle should take you one minute to complete. But if you wanna sleep tonight, you'd better do it in forty-five seconds. Is that clear? I've got a Marine-issue stopwatch that is more accurate than a Hellfire missile so when I say 'go' you better move!"

We didn't have to deal with much reluctance that day. They all did great and as a whole we came out ahead of a lot of the other platoons. However, they still did not get to sleep much that night because not everyone completed the A-Frame in forty-five seconds. In my walkthrough at 0200, I found a few who were not at the position of attention, so I dumped them out of their racks. No slack is given just because you're tired. But I was proud of them.

I remember

When I was in boot camp and first observed the obstacles at the Confidence Course in Sand Diego, they scared me to death. I had always pictured Marines as being unstoppable champions and unparalleled athletes and I did not see myself that way at all. Lord, I remember thinking, here's where I'm going to be seen for what I really am. As it turns out, I did just fine. I was capable of more than I'd imagined. Others that I went through training with had a much stronger sense of self but I was gaining mental strength with each victory.

And let me share this because it might help somebody: the CC helped me master my fears, but it never entirely erased them. I recall my best friend saying, as he conquered every challenge, "I have no fear! I have power, love and a sound mind". I've never had a problem jumping out of an airplane, but put me thirty or forty feet off the ground and I still get nervous, to this day. I don't enjoy standing on the top end of a telephone pole, though I've done it many times. From 3,000 feet in the air you have time to make corrections. From 30 feet you don't.

That's just me.

As a DI, I had to recertify every three months. I had to repeatedly face those same challenges over and over again; the CC, the fighting skills, the physical fitness tests; it's vital for a DI to do as much and more than he demands of his recruits. A Parris Island credo goes: "Let's be darn sure no man's ghost will ever say, if my training had only done its job."

But it's never been as hard as that first time.

"You can keep your Army khaki
You can keep your Navy blue
I have the world's best fighting man,
To introduce to you

His uniform is different
The best you've ever seen
The German's called him 'Devil Dog'
His real name is 'Marine'."

Private Tawes
(The little puke)

A few cycles had gone by and my face had hardened permanently into a scowl and my squint had been cemented by observing the endless dopey antics of new recruits. Sweat had become my second skin, an armor that repelled the effects of sun, bugs, and time, but never discolored my green creased perfection in the presence of those I trained. The recruits ate and slept more than I did but I never let it show. Truth be told I was always more tired, more frazzled, more hoarse, more bruised, and more stressed than they ever were. But those were feelings and I had learned not to let them crawl up out of me like the dreaded sand fleas that leached from our training beaches.

My quiet, private moments were rare, as my days were often 20 hours long. So I consumed them quickly like big, numbing gulps of whiskey, packing as much as I could into the small spots of time.

I'd pull over by a marshy cove at 0200 every once in awhile and talk to Jesus while I skimmed stones across the rippling mirror at alligator's heads. Occasionally a stone would hit something and a splash would follow, so I must've hit a few with my little, flying stones.

Sometimes my wife and I would barbeque or leave the island for a quick dinner. But I was seldom more than four of five hours away from my next shift.

Taw-ezzz

It didn't matter what a new recruit's background had been—they were all soft. All of them. Some came from prestigious civilian organizations—swat teams, college athletic programs, and corporate internships. Others came from gangs and an unusually high percentage came straight from the comfy apple pie world of grandma's high school daycare center where everything was always ok and every situation had a bandage just the right size. Yeah.

I'd reflect back to the time I met my own drill instructors. I'd been in awe of how sharp they looked. Their creases looked like razors and I'll never forget how their Smokey Bear cover cut their eyeballs in two. I was very conscious in my efforts to emulate them; I wanted to set that very same example for my own recruits.

But it usually took the whole three months of training for my disgust to alchemize into pride. Midway through, their potential was manifesting but it would be longer before I'd feel satisfied I'd done my job. At their graduations I'd wonder, whose life did I save? Which of these recruits will face combat and run from it? Which ones will charge the ambush and take out the enemy?

There was one recruit in my current platoon that stood out. Tawes was his name. He seemed to respond to my relentless shadowing and punishments the way a drill instructor wants his recruits to respond—with change. He seemed to buckle properly to the character building that repetitious torments proposed.

I called him "my little motorboat." His season under my tender guidance was a rainy one, so he spent many hours in a horizontal position face down in a mud puddle blowing bubbles.

"Taw-ezzzzz," I'd yell, exaggerating the "ezz." "Don't you move a millimeter." I'd press my boot against the back of his grape and wait a second or two after the bubbles quit before releasing him.

"Who owns you, you little puke?

"Sir, the Marine Corps, Sir!"

"So, who controls when you breathe in and when you breathe out?"

"Sir, Drill Instructor Sergeant McDugle, SIR!"

He'd never flinch or panic when he ran out of air. He learned that I'd let my boot up just at the right time. His trust in his drill instructors was implicit.

You might be thinking, so you say, but how would Tawes tell the story?

I'll let him speak for himself. Let me introduce you to Recruit Tawes:

My first day of training was on the fourth of July. I'll never forget it as long as I live. I turned eighteen just a few days earlier at the Recruit Receiving section of Support Battalion, where my short stay flashed by in a blur. Hardly any sleep. Hardly any peace. Then, myself and eighty or so other young men, were formed into Platoon 1014, 1st Recruit Training Battalion, Charlie Company. What a motley bunch we were—loose, stupid, and extremely nervous about what we'd gotten ourselves into. The receiving drill instructors constantly tormented us while pounding overwhelming quantities of information into our brains. The repetition was mind numbing:

"Repeat my ditty! Scream it, recruit! OPEN YOUR DISGUSTING MOUTH!"

On the third day, we met our Senior Drill Instructor, Staff Sergeant Martin, a guy who looked like he'd been through twelve wars. I've never forgotten his pitted, leathery face. After his speech, we were turned over to his drill instructors, Sergeant Death ***(McDugle)*** *and Sergeant Destruction* ***(Flannary)****—two green lightning bolts with big mouths. They had real names, of course, but they were never uttered by us. That would've been sacrilegious. "Sir" was how we addressed* *them, when we dared. And few dared. If there had been such a thing as stealth combat vests, we would've paid a million dollars for one. There were no places to hide from these guys.*

Everything that happens on Parris Island happens at the speed of light. There is absolutely no down time. Immediately, we were marched to the parade deck by Sergeant Death, a trek haunted by the spectra of Sergeant Destruction who had perfected the art of materializing out of thin air. We were blasted for every minor drill infraction. If your arm swung an inch too far, he'd notice.

"Six to the front, three to the rear. SWING YOUR ARMS, RECRUIT! Forty inches back to the chest!" Perfection, though it seemed unachievable, was the demand. Every movement had been crafted by the marine's architects and recorded in some remote chapter of the Book of Knowledge, which the drill instructors had apparently memorized from cover to cover. Who were these guys?

Sergeant Death led the way, as he would nearly all the time, his shoulders rigid as a beam and his brow granite. I DID NOT WANT HIM TO TURN AROUND! It meant he had read somebody's mind and God had whispered the merciless judgment for our sins in his ear. And man, it was hot! I swear Satan himself was trying to fan off the heat, looking for shade on the bleachers overlooking the parade deck. We were drenched in sweat.

Suddenly, Sergeant Death spun around and parked us on a patch of pavement. He promptly issued a command that we had just learned:

"Ready…"

To this day, when I hear the preparatory command, "READY…" my mind screams "one-oh-one-four!" and spikes with adrenalized anticipation of the follow up.

"SEAT!"

"Drop like a rock!" was our unified response, as we plummeted with precision to the sitting position of at attention. Right down onto that hot military tar or lava. That's how it felt, anyway. Our butts burned from the searing heat but every attempt to alleviate the discomfort drew Sergeant Destruction's attention. I wanted to pour water from my canteen around my waist and onto my thighs but the sound of him verbally maiming other recruits for similar attempts struck fear into me. And Sergeant Death was always in my periphery; both of them were everywhere, all the time. I don't know where they learned to do that but their trainers had been masters!

After what seemed like hours of instruction and correction, the sun went down. Finally. Would this day ever end? Did these guys ever turn off?

Death & Destruction

So we sat there.

I can still smell the pungent night air. It was a mixture of natural and unnatural odors as the island released the growth and the rot of its leafy soul into the humidity. And we were releasing our own reek as well. I call it "recruit stench" It's the combined waft of sweaty private areas, bad breath, and the god-awful smell that 782 gear emits when human sweat contaminates it. The military needs to work on that one. It was stifling.

Suddenly a band started playing. What the...?

The spot lit blacktop around us filled with commotions and footsteps and trumpets and a cacophony of other indistinguishable sounds, both near and far off. Parris Island didn't shut down at five o'clock; in fact, **its** *purple black sky amplified even the most distant of sounds, of which there were many.*

But we were told not to move, so we didn't move. Not a muscle. Our eyes remained locked straight ahead.

When the band finished playing, I heard the soft clump-clump-clump of a small group of marchers, who I could tell were just to the left and behind us.

Some orders were given and then I heard what sounded like the swish of rifles being spun, although quieter and smoother than I'd ever pictured a weapon could be handled. The rhythm made us sleepy, a dangerous thing.

Once in awhile a recruit would tilt just slightly—you could tell he was nodding off – but Death or Destruction were on him instantly, threatening to superglue his eyelids open. Or make him stand on one foot for twelve hours. Could they do that? I was starting to think there were no limits.

Then, finally, things started to quiet down. The magical rifle-spinners marched off to whatever corner of the gator nest they'd come from and we prepared to march back to our squad bay. Little did I know I'd just witnessed (without seeing) the famed Silent Drill Team, an elite twenty-four man exhibition unit that travels the world representing the Marine Corps.

But right then I didn't really care. I didn't even care if we ate or not. My rack was waiting with dreams of tennis shoes and t-shirts and fishing and my girlfriend. Not necessarily in that order.

Our bodies were stiff, so our march was still, and boy did they let us know it. I thought maybe their vocal chords were made out of belt leather. I wondered if Sergeant Death and Destruction would still sound the same after a few weeks of hollering at us. That was the dumbest question I'd ever thought!

So ended Day One.

The cosmic balance

Drill Instructors and their recruits never get to know each other. A DIs effectiveness would be diminished if things got personal. However, occasionally you recognize individuals that, under other circumstances, you might invite home for a barbeque. Natural leaders are discerned instantly. Great followers are recognized also. They're both important and both can be improved with training.

In a three-month span, a recruit's individuality will surface; his sense of humor will come to light, his stoicism and his loyalty. And all the characteristics of a recruit, with few exceptions, can become an asset to the Corps with honing.

On a battlefield, the unique DNA of a platoon forms a whole wherein one man's strength balances the weakness of another.

That cosmic balance forms itself naturally and the puzzle pieces join at the appropriate time, but boot-camp is not the time. Boot camp is stripping down time so a DI keeps his distance emotionally from the men he's training, though he might like to know them better.

And besides, dishing it out can be fun!

Blood was spilled

A hand came out of nowhere and grabbed me by the facemask of my helmet. Sergeant Death sent me flying towards the open end of the tunnel, screaming "KILL HIM TAW-EZZ!"

He called me "Taw-ezz" just because he could, I guess.

"Sir, yes SIR!" I shouted, plunging into the gigantic, ribbed pipe. At the other end, two recruits were waiting for me with pugil sticks—heavily padded poles, almost like martial arts staffs. I exited the tunnel with all the ramming power I could muster but they were braced for me. Wham! I took a blow to the face. Then wham-wham-wham! I had a pugil stick too and landed blows of my own, knocking the weapon out of the hand of one.

"Kill him recruit, kill him!" screamed our Senior DI, who was making a rare appearance. He seemed to intersect us at pivotal points in our training, like a bulldog with a modicum of benevolence. He could be harsh, but would occasionally dish out a personal compliment and even inquire about us on a personal level. He was our big, bad granddaddy!

Well, I fought but I got whooped in the end. One marine against two other marines, similarly trained, is a tough deal. But part of boot camp is learning to take it, not just give it.

And to this day, I'm not sure if the Senior DI was encouraging those guys or me, but it doesn't really matter. Blood was spilled, pain was incurred, and skills were learned. And that's what counts.

Hygiene

Hygiene inspection was always a treat when Sergeant Destruction had the detail. I can still recall the cold steel of his NCO sword pressing just below my right ear as he instructed me on the proper length of sideburns.

"They shall not extend beyond the orifice of the ear, Taw-ezz! The orifice of the ear!"

He was a scary looking dude. When he was in your face, staring into your soul, it seemed like he had no pupils; just gunmetal colored discs welded to the whites of his eyes.

And he had a tattoo on his right forearm-a snake coiled around an NCO sword. I sometimes wondered if it wasn't the true "mark-of-the-beast," versus the traditional "666."

In the background, I could hear Sergeant Death destroying the squad bay. Canteens and mattresses were flying through the air. Footlockers were being dumped over. A window broke.

We had heard that the DIs referred to this havoc wreaking as a "tornado" but we had another name for it, "the bridge over troubled waters." It was a favorite activity of both of our drill instructors. Our common prayer was, "Dear God, please don't let it happen tonight."

They could never be second-guessed though. It was better to just be ready.

Oops!

Recruit Boone, Collins, and myself were all assigned to the same stick during Day Movement training. Some DI whose name I've forgotten had been assigned as our instructor. He wore gold jump wings and a scuba bubble on his uniform and apparently thought enough of himself to tutor us on the difference between "Recon," which had been his Marine outfit before becoming a drill instructor, and "Anglico."

By the end of that particularly muggy, uniform drenching day, the whole platoon had been rehearsed according to his whim. Recons are better than Anglicos. Got it? Okay, yeah...we got it!

"What are Anglicos?" he shouted.

"Wannabe Recons, SIR!" we responded. There was more, and we memorized the whole call-and-response as instructed. Little did we realize the woe our obedience would bring us until it was too late.

When Sergeant Death came for us that evening, we were ordered to repeat the performance for him, which we did, at the top of our lungs, like any Marine worth his salt. Only, as we performed, it evoked a glare and fire in Sergeant Death's eyes that I'd never seen before. We paid. Oh boy, did we pay. In the pit, in the squad bay, and in OT the next morning. And every second in between.

It turns out that Sergeant Death was a proud Anglico Marine. Anglico are a special forces Marine branch consisting of small ops units who perform surveillance and call in fire support, often behind enemy lines. They experience a high degree of wartime action. So he bristled at weakness. Any sign of it, in anyone. And he was furious at what had been drilled into our heads about his former unit.

Pain was dispensed like bubblegum out of a machine.

Personally, I think the whole Anglico versus Recon thing was a private running joke between Sergeant Death and the other DI. A back-and-forth banter that played out at the recruit's expense and that behind the scenes they were really good friends.

But I don't know that for sure. Even now.

DI Song

We were taunted constantly, assured that we would all die overseas and that there were guys named "Jody" in our hometowns that would inherit all of our girlfriends.

I can't tell you how many nights I woke up in excruciating pain, my legs cramping from the countless monkey humpers that Sergeants Death and Destruction made me do.

But Sergeant Death had a song that he'd sing when he'd relieve Sergeant Destruction from the tedious vocal task that entailed his billet on one of our hikes. My mind would be racing with the day's lessons (what is the kill radius of an M-67 fragmentation grenade and what are the five most common types of battlefield wounds?) when his proud voice took over.

"Don't let the green grass fool ya
Don't let it change your mind
No, don't let the green grass fool ya
Don't let it change your mind
Here we going to 1st Phase
Don't let the green grass fool ya
Rifle Range, Rifle Range, here we come

Don't let it change your mind
Rifle Range, now here we come
Oh Mess Night, here we come
Don't let the green grass fool ya
Here we come BWT
Don't let it change your mind
Oh uh, here we come Graduation
Don't let the green grass fool ya
Sing it for me, one more time
Don't let it change your mind"

Until the day I die, I think the soothing song of my drill instructor rising into the dust or into the first stars of evening, transcending the pain and chaos of the moment, will be counted as one of the most beautiful things I've ever heard in my life.

Last warning Tawes

If I was still his drill instructor, I'd probably bust his chops for that—for being so poetic about something as magnificently rare and raw as the song of a drill instructor who knows who he is under the gaze of God and who has drank from the same cup of agony as those he trains.

But I'm not.

I know very little about Recruit Tawes personally, even to this day, and what I do know is barely more than you know. I do know that he was trained to survive and kill. The eight pages of recollections he sent me for this book tells most of it.

He informed me that he had gone on to become a Drill Instructor and I'd like to let him know, right now, publicly, that I'm proud of him.

And that Anglico/Recon stuff, Sergeant Tawes—I know you remember learning that Anglico is always better than recon.

The bird head incident

The Marine Corps instills a sense of belonging to something much greater than ourselves. We are legendary and know it, but not arrogantly. That particularly dangerous and undignified trait of arrogance has been bred out of us. "Trained confidence" better describes our disposition.

History is filled with stories of a few Marines holding off or killing hundreds with little more than a rifle, a bayonet, and some grenades. Our main saber has always been our mental strength, and its sheath, brotherhood. A Marine watches out for the man next to him and becomes ten for the sake of one if he has to. He's been thoroughly trained how to do exactly that—how to become more than he is.

There is a nickname – "Devil Dog" – for the camouflaged ghost that traverses terrain like the air itself, inhabiting the topography of danger's domain like he its rightful owner. It suits us just fine.

The term comes from the notorious "Battle of Belleau Wood" during which a German horde had surrounded three hundred or so entrenched and weary Marines. The situation looked grim through the smoky and noxious fog coughed up by the enemy artillery emissions, but there's always light at the end of the tunnel if that tunnel is the barrel of a marine's weapon.

The Germans pressed, but the Marines held, and held, and impossibly held.

Eventually, an advance had to be made, through waist-high grass while pelted by spitting lead.

As the Marines stepped out, their German commanders, lapping furiously at the bloody chalice of victory and intoxicated by its dangling bait, urged their own tired troops to rise for the kill, but a lone voice deflated the din of battle-roar and focused the Marines' commitment:

"Come on, you sons of bitches, do you want to live forever?"

This was the shout of Gunnery Sergeant Dan Daly as his battalion charged forward. The fighting was fierce and became close-quartered many times. Bayonet clashed against bayonet and fist grappled throat during the hellish engagement. Marines were shot and fell only to get back up again and go on the charge.

Eventually a foothold was gained, and, although the battle would continue for many more days, the legend of American Marines as "Teufel Hunden," or Devil Dogs—fighters who kept getting back up after they'd been shot—had been established.

Recruit Bobbins

Drill instructors wear many hats under the one the recruit sees. Besides being warrior makers, we are mentors and classroom teachers—history being one of our favorite subjects. Each recruit needs to assimilate lore and lineage into his mental DNA so that he truly understands who he is and who he is becoming. My best friend knew exactly who he was and that very knowledge made His decision making much easier. Spiritual blood must flow from one to the next to the next, through veins of heritage and under the guardianship and alchemy of a Drill Instructor's tutorial. It is true that we were born at Parris Island the land that God forgot.

Beyond us, experience waits.

I understood from the beginning—all drill instructors do—that I was responsible for much more than just conditioning young men physically and mentally…I was to inform them. And that is a task! I was responsible for their life and their survival in the worst times of their lives.

Ninety percent of what a recruit learns in boot camp has nothing to do with his weapon or his night vision goggles or how to survive in the field for extended periods of time. How a man carries himself and conducts his affairs outside of combat will determine the type of man he is in combat. A Marine is on duty 24 hours a day seven days a week and 365 days a year.

So, if you really want to make a drill instructor mad—if you really want to pop his insignias loose—just joke around about anything having to do with the Marine Corps family tree and its heroes and traditions. Treat it lightly. Doodle in class and let your mind wander. After all, you can bench press three-hundred pounds. You can even beat half the platoon in arm-wrestling.

Let me warn you, though…

A DI knows the glazed look of boredom and can smell "I don't care."

You will memorize everything he instructs you to and you will learn to recite it verbatim.

"It's not bell-owww wood,' Recruit Snavely, it's bell-oh wood! Are you deaf, dumb, and blind? Do you have ass holes for ears?

"Sir, no SIR!"

I hated it when their minds wandered, or when they seemed disinterested. Somehow, the occasional recruit is able to learn an amazing trick; I've seen it dozens of times. They'll be standing at attention; heels together, eyes piercing and brow furrowed—the perfect spot on picture of a

Marine—and yet be fast asleep! I call it the Houdini limb-lock.

But I had a cure for that.

I had special incentive training techniques for those who exhibited non-medical Attention Deficit Disorders.

"Recruit Bobbins! RECRUIT BOBBINS!"

"S-s-sir, yes SIR!"

"Were you sleeping Recruit Bobbins?"

Sir, no SIR! Sir, this recruit had sweat in his eyes and they were stinging, SIR!"

"Recruit Bobbins, how can you sweat when we're not even moving? I wanna know what you look like when you REALLY sweat. Let's go give the sand fleas a drink…"

Spraying water on a sand pit drives the fleas to the surface where they'll hop like jumping beans onto the nearest victim. And man oh man, were their little mandibles fierce.

Recruit Bobbins became a history major, I'm proud to say. In fact, he made my honor roll! Other recruits were tossed out of their position as their body was launched from its nice comfy sleeping position.

Princess Schmoe

Nobody likes an angry drill instructor, except for another drill instructor. He'll jump on the bandwagon with the first DI go for the ride, and don't you know, all hell will break loose!

Someone once asked how to tell when a DI is really mad - they always look grumpy.

Well, here's how it works.

When we're introduced to new recruits for the first time, we've already got our "angry" turned on. It's pretty much what we have to do to break a recruit. But the show and the fun and the howdy-doody wears off pretty quickly. Then we get pissed when we get gaffed off by some asshole recruit that knows more than we do.

The recruits don't pay attention and do things the way we want them done and our patience wears thin. They act like they smoked all the dope in Colombia and stored the resins in their head-fat. It's something else. You can demonstrate to them over and over again the proper way to make their racks or fold their socks or even the direction they should twist a Q-tip in their ear-hole, but you know you're going to have to do it again. The information overload short-circuits their civilian wiring and pea sized brains. So, before long, you're tired of repeating yourself...tired of explaining the same exact thing you just told the recruit standing right in front of them. And from that point on—until the cycle is nearly over—you're a mean, impatient, demanding Son of a bitch. This tactic of repeating yourself hundreds of times is the way recruits learn. Eventually they catch on.

But when a drill instructor loses it completely—passes the point of control and knows it—he leaves the recruits and heads for the DI hut, where he can vent and throw staplers and language around and curse the day American's mothers gave birth to his platoon. Rarely does a recruit witness this phenomenon, although they surely will get rolled up on by its after effects.

Occasionally though, and I share this with hesitancy, an outburst will erupt where it shouldn't and in front of whom it shouldn't.

I recall such an instance:

Drill Instructor Sergeant Schaffer was a stocky DI who filled a uniform to the seams when he put it on. He had a stiff face with features that were so fused together a handful of stoic expressions got him through a day's activities splendidly. As a matter of fact, I think his bag of tricks contained a scowl, a wince, and a smirk. That's it. He kept the rest at home, probably in the lettuce drawer of his fridge where the things least needed in life lay dormant.

He came to the drill field a year after me but we became fast friends, having much in common. He loved to train recruits hardcore and was relentless in his dedication. He didn't need much sleep, ate as fast as he could (when he ate) and remained with his recruits until something out of his control peeled him away. He was a great DI. He had this wonderful ability—something I've always admire in drill instructors—to spit fire the minute he opened his mouth. It was an effortless thing for him.

So, late one evening (an unusually brisk one for the season) he lost his cool. I don't remember what the catalyst had been, but I witnessed the results. The wind was whipping through the palm trees outside, but a full blown hurricane had hit the squad bay and was bettering our little green sprouts!

Shit flew everywhere and, although I'd seen it a hundred times before, I was amazed at what a single drill instructor could do to the home of seventy or eighty recruits, in a very, very short amount of time.

I could not stand by idle so I decided to join in on the hurricane. So we were in tandem—a perfectly tuned dynamo of destruction.

Then, out of the corner of my eye, I noticed him pause beside a recruit's rack and begin to rail at him because he wasn't moving fast enough. This particular recruit was a repeat offender. He was a big guy, so visits to the pit and the quarterdeck hadn't fazed him either—nothing seemed to penetrate the thick callous this guy called a head. That's when Schaffer blew…

"You fucking' bitch of a baby!" he screamed. "Do you want me to send you over to the WM (Women Marine) side of the island? I can get a training bra and a hairpin for you and march your ass around until even the alligators are wondering what you are. Is that what you want me to do, recruit?"

"Sir, no SIR!" answered Recruit Schmoe.

"Are you SURE recruit? Because I will, I swear by the hair your mama saved in your baby book, I will. I'll make it so your whore of a mama wouldn't even recognize what she gave birth to, Princess Schmoe—she'll wonder if you're a boy or a girl! And what the hell are your BOOTS DOING DOWN THERE?"

Uh-oh. A pair of boots sticking out from under a rack is always in the wrong place.

I watched Sergeant Schaffer grab the pair in question. He launched the first one at Schmoe and hit him square in the gut, the second he launched with all his might—not at anyone or anything in particular, although a few heads wisely ducked—and then noticed the porthole (window) it was headed for.

I knew if the boot hit the porthole and broke the glass, we'd be in for it. Investigators would come around and very likely we'd be charged with terrorizing recruits, or damaging government property, at the very least, if they couldn't generate enough evidence to push the more serious violations through.

I watched that boot fly end over end in slow motion toward my worst fear. Then...relief. I caught the flash of its polished toe as it snagged on the top pole of a rack and slammed to the floor with a skidding "thwaaaaack!"

Whew!

It's possible to maintain a disgusted look while exhibiting shock, which is the combined countenance that both Sergeant Schaffer and I wore. But our near panic remained concealed from the recruits as we demonstrated the art of plasticity.

Yup, a close call and a couple of lessons learned:

Don't throw anything a hundred miles an hour at a porthole.

The gut of a recruit is a much better place for the leather to land. The thump of leather on a recruit has an unusually stabilizing effect on troublesome platoons.

Pit Stop

The next morning we all had a good laugh about the incident, but inside I think everybody felt a renewed sense of caution. Keep in check. Stay in control. These were our unspoken but common thoughts.

Little did we realize that we would soon witness an even more extreme tirade. Nothing illegal, mind you, but maybe it should've been. The natural order of things was about to be disrupted to the shock and horror of recruits and drill instructors alike. Some would be tempted to laugh and some would retch. Some…well, some just wouldn't sleep so good that night.

But it was still early and we were all in good humor as we set off, the rising sun splashing our faces with its warm cheer. The marshes were quiet and the air was filled with the familiar clomp-clomp-clomp of the island's booted heartbeat. A mix of military vehicles and civilian vehicles convoyed back and forth on the main road nearby—we could just see them behind a jagged line of palms—indicating the base was hosting guests that day. There were press days and there were political days and occasionally guided tours crossed our paths, especially on Fridays, which were graduation days.

Personally, I didn't like having so many people around; kids, moms, girls, and dads ogling us like we were animals in a cage. It was very distracting, as was the boisterous conversations of political entourages. I just didn't like it and often thought that San Diego's fortress type environment (San Diego was where I'd done my own basic training) provided a better vacuum to create Marines in.

The recruits filed in and out of the chow hall with great precision. By now they were dialed in to the daily routine and even the knuckleheads among them were finding their rhythm. They were starting to look like identical cousins, the whole bunch of them. Color, race, and creed belonged to the outside world and not to Marines. Heading toward the squad bay to change into the PT gear, they moved like a machine…a big, organic one with power to spare.

Only—oh shit, there's always something.

One of the recruits had a button unbuttoned, the third one down from his collar. And just enough of his t-shirt was poking through to tick me off! In a flash, I grabbed the guy by that protruding bit of white cotton and skin, which I stretched until half his undershirt was hanging down his chest. He gave me the new recruit terror look—the "uh-oh" face that one adopts when their perfection is found wanting.

We happened to be right by the pit, so we ordered the recruits to halt and proceeded to perform a quick inspection, which, needless to say, supplied us with a few more untidy specimens to toss into the sand.

The Pit is a sand pit, usually twelve feet wide by twelve feet across, that decorates both ends of a squad bay near the ladder well (stairs). They all have them, and though their purposes are paramount, we give them very little maintenance. Some have sand spurs while others are littered with pebbles. Some are damp and shaded, but others faster In the Carolina sun. And on Parris Island, they all have sand fleas. Its where, among other things, DIs turns recruits into sugar cookies.

First we get them real sweaty by sending them back and forth on some pull-up bars followed by a series of push-ups and side-straddle hops. Then we order them to bury themselves in the sand, the goal being to exit The Pit with as little skin visible as possible. They'd better have sand in their mouths and noses and ears or they would be sent back in to roll around some more.

"You'd better look like a cat turd in a litter box," Sergeant Schaffer would holler, "except alive and moving!"

Recruits hated spending time in the pit getting "thrashed," which is what we called pit sessions, so it's a highly effective training tool. Exercising and running and even marches can be grueling but there's nothing as miserable as being exhausted and dirty and bug-bitten at the same time.

Yes, it was a messy ordeal.

But it taught the recruits to develop an eye for detail. It taught them to scrutinize and square each other away and got their eyes off themselves and onto the bigger picture.

Kicking up dust

"Fall in," I ordered, after the thrashing was over. "When I dismiss you, I want you all to change into your PT gear. And you turd clumps brush each other off before you enter my squad bay and you better do it like Mr. Clean because if I see ONE GRAIN of sand on my deck, everybody's going to play pit games today!

They were smart recruits. They had the firewatch recruits pass their PT clothes out to them and fell back into formation a few minutes later, still gritty and grimy but willing to endure for the sake of their green brethren.

Then off we marched.

Our senior DI had asked that we finish the day's PT with a run, so our plan was set.

Before long, we were kicking up dust on the circuit course. Leading the run, I made sure our platoon maintained an appropriate distance between the other platoons and, more importantly, that every recruit sounded off cadence at the top of his lungs.

Poor little bird

We were probably three miles into the island's circuit course when I called to the recruits to route step, which is a slow walk. Then we covered maybe another half a mile for a cool-down lap before forming over our canteens for a drink of water. I'd give them two or three minutes to cool-down before we began the trek back.

A couple other platoons had followed us on the trail and had broke to a rest right behind our platoon, so all of us DIs were bantering back and forth, slamming each other's recruits and even barking into each other's bone yards a bit.

The recruits always tensed when an unfamiliar drill instructor started to berate them. They were somewhat used to their own but never knew what to think about somebody else's. It would be like one dad letting another dad punish his kids. It's not natural, and we knew it could upset the dynamics of a recruit's psychology, so, except for the occasional prank, we seldom crossed each other's authoritative lines.

I was chuckling at a joke—a rather derogatory statement I'd made about a friend's unusually short-statured platoon—when I noticed one of the other DIs peering into the swamp grass. He had heard something and upon closer examination found a bird's nest containing several noisy babies—little scrawny things. And they were probably lice ridden.

If I haven't mentioned it yet, or haven't finished the portrait completely, drill instructors can also be showmen, some more than others. There is an ongoing but friendly competition between DIs and their platoons, ultimately showcased in the drill competitions and the comparisons of event scores, so different occasions can prompt a drill instructor to demonstrate his raw and primal gutsiness in a spectacular display.

And the most common scenario for this occurrence is when multiple platoons are gathered together, as we presently were.

The circumstances were ripe for heroic demonstrations.

So this drill instructor (I don't recall his name), heady no doubt from his morning coffee and from the endorphins released by our run, proceeded to lift a baby swallow from its nest, raising it in a clenched fist for all to see. He certainly had everybody's attention.

"Aint nothing in life," he belted out, "you can't do, if, you put your mind to it. If you've got 20 enemies surrounding you and all you have to eat is a frog, then you better go on and eat that frog. If your drill instructor tells you you're going to march two hundred miles on a diet of crickets, then you better quit thinking about apple pie and start thanking God for cricket guts! The phrase, 'I can't do THAT' should not exist in a Marine's mind!"

And with that, he bit the head off the bird and spat it to the ground, tossing the body over his shoulder like an amulet. The chirping stopped.

I thought he was going to throw up, but he didn't. He held it together.

The recruits were frozen. Nobody said a word, but I could see some nervously choking back the contents of their stomachs, so I ordered our platoon into formation and ran them into forgetfulness.

I'm okay with a lot of stuff, but I could feel my own stomach churning. Boy, I thought…that guy is nuts!

Did his weird little act impart anything valuable into the recruits that were present? Frankly, I don't know. If anything, maybe Sergeant Schaffer and I were the beneficiaries. After that we felt more okay about our own balance—we were hard but not freaky-hard and were conscientious about our methods. Our platoons exited our guardianship with their grapes on their shoulders and knew Marine reality for what it was, without distortion.

As for the bird-eater…I didn't know the guy well, but he seemed to graduate some sharp Marines and was still training when I left Parris Island. My guess is he had an impulsive moment, and made the best of it after realizing what he'd done. He probably mixed his gin and tonic with Listerine that night, swearing to his wife that the red on his collar was not lipstick.

Either way, I'm sure his recruits never forgot him as they advanced into their Marine careers with the knowledge that if you're in a tough spot and hungry and a bird is all you have to eat—it aint gonna kill ya!

"Mama, Mama, can't you see?
What the Marine Corps done to me
They sat me down in the chair
When I looked I had not hair
Mama, Mama, can't ya see?
What the Marine Corps done to me
I used to drive a Chevrolet
But now I march around all day
Mama, Mama, can't you see?
What the Marine Corps done to me
I used to drive a Cadillac
Now I carry one on my back
Mama, Mama, can't you see?
What the Marine Corps done to me
Cut my hair and shaved my face

Made me a part of the human race.
Mama, Mama, can't you see?
What the Marine Corps done to me
I'm walking tall and feeling good
I'm doing things I never thought I could."

"**A** yellow birdie with a yellow bill
Landed on my window sill
Lured him in with a piece of bread
Then I crushed his freakin' head"

Summer on Parris Island

The title "Marine," when not only earned, but kept, is a title that distinguishes a man or a woman as part of an elite, worldwide organization. At any given moment, the Marines have fewer members than IBM has employees, and it's a stressful a job as any on the planet. More responsibility is placed on a young E4 Marine Corporal than on an Army E6, but because of budget limitations, the Marines cannot promote fast enough those who deserve pay grades far above their job descriptions.

Combat situations aside, a drill instructor's job is the toughest of them all.

So "liberty" (a Marine's temporary time off) is like a rare choice morsel to a DI. It's like a piece of steak—wonderfully flavored but tough to chew sometimes, because although it's essential and fun, it breaks our stride. We're used to living by the clock and by the letter, and liberty is a sort of temporary freedom; there are no clocks and no book to tell you what to do and how to do it.

How do you relax?

How do you make your body and your mind switch gears on a dime?

You can't tell your wife you love her in cadence and you can't march your kids to their cereal bowls and expect to maintain a healthy, happy home life. But a drill instructor is not a rubber band so we tend to stay taut unless we find an equalizer—something that will forcefully massage our stresses away and short circuit our wiring temporarily.

Some are blessed with spouses that love them unconditionally and have zero tolerance for dictatorship in the home. The coveted DI cover is set aside until he (or she) leaves to report back in again.

Others aren't so fortunate.

They have no one and own very little. Their only families are their fellow DIs and the recruit changelings that exist as a blur of faces in a procession of cycles.

For many of these, alcohol becomes the massage therapist—dulling moisture they can drizzle onto their brain synapses to bring respite from anchored thought patterns.

Fortunately, I fell into the middle of these categories, although some days I wished I was wholly in the one or the other, because there are a lot of unknowns in the often bland centers of things where even the medicine of reassurances vacillate like the Atlantic's teasing shore winds.

I had a wife, and loved her, and she loved me too, but the stresses of the corps took its toll on both of us.

But we did the best we knew at the time, and it was adequate. My springs got enough uncoiling that when it came time to re-don the military chasses, I could shoulder it.

The Land that God forgot

Marines call Parris Island the "land that God forgot."

Drive the causeway into its scrubby, tree moss entrance, one time and you'll know why. There's a beauty to it, for sure, but it's that kind of Eastern seaboard beauty that seduces with its palm trees while preparing its ambushes in the lower elements of a thicket. I'm talking about the island itself, mind you. The base has been entrenched there long enough for its toeholds to turn into roots and its paved concourses into island skin.

If you were going in as a recruit, the first evidence that there's no turning back, besides the watery expanse you're getting ready to cross, is The Guard Shack. I capitalize it because although there are others on the base, this particular one is the jugular of them all. Approaching it can almost seem like a Twilight Zone moment. Reality narrows to the gaps between the pupils of the Marines on duty, who don't miss a thing going out or coming in, and who possibly have archangel wings tucked flatly under their pressed, khaki shirts.

My wife would marvel at their professionalism. The shack, the gates, and the Marines on duty were both the business card and the force field of the whole place. I've always been professional when traveling through the gate ready for them when I pulled up, ID in hand, to them a drill instructor was what they dealt with daily. Their professional appearance and "Thank you, Sergeant" along with a wave on through added to the professional attitude of the island.

Maybe Sergeant Destruction had been their boot camp instructor.

After passing the sentinels, if you were a recruit on a bus loaded with others, your nirvana preconceptions would begin to evaporate almost immediately after leaving the blue stretch of water you just crossed. Suddenly you find yourself shuttled down a two lane road between rows of ancient moss-drenched and gravity-burdened **trees**, whose dreariness clamps onto your soul so strongly you might wish you hadn't chosen a window seat to view your exit from all you've ever known.

Yes, when the scenery turns primordial and the revelation that not all islands are a paradise sinks in, a swelling of the throat and the steam from your fear may lubricate the hot smudge where your cheek presses the window glass.

Don't let anyone else see, though. Your reputation is on the line.

Once you've penetrated the island proper, you're isolation's pretty much complete. Ocean and swamp water and alligators surround you, and the roars and groans of the latter will become your bedtime sing-stresses. Later, after you've done your time on the island and moved on, you'll even have a hard time sleeping without their incessant taunting, for a while anyway. And when you get older, you'll probably bore your kids and grandkids with your fond memories of boot camp as you show them your dulling belt buckle and pictures your parents took at graduation. The faces of those who stood around you still bring to remembrance their names, last names at least.

"And Sergeant Death, you'll tell them, he was quite the terror. Oh…he could be hard! But he loved us, you know. He didn't show it much, but we could tell he did; our cycle was his favorite. I'll never forget his face and I guarantee you he remembers ours, each one of us!"

Whoever you are, I won't bust your bubble.

If you're dreaming and waxing nostalgic, just go ahead and keep right on…

No escape

A recruit is warned immediately upon arrival not to try to leave the island in any but a procedural way. In other words, don't try to escape by swimming—you'll die on the waves, beaten by the rocks, or gators. No one's ever gotten off successfully that way.

Better not try slacking either. The Marine Corps is a patient organization and perfectly willing to start a recruit all over again; we won't let one go for being slow or stupid or weak; they're just marked as needing extra care and attention.

Nope, if a recruit sets his mind on leaving and determines to either act up or give up, he's in for more of an adventure than he would've had if he'd suck it up and stuck with the original 13-week program.

I've painted a bleak picture, haven't I? What a horrendous place, you must be thinking. But I did say, if you'll read back just a bit, is that there is a beauty to it—you just don't comprehend it until you've forgotten everything your mind's attic has stored for comparison; your mom and dad's back yard; your grandparent's vacation cabin in Estes Park; the brisk, fall air of a high school football game…

Get those things out of your mind and you're good.

The brochures given by recruiters to potentials—the shiny ones with the magazine quality photographs of recruits firing rifles under sunny blue skies—do portray a very real side of the Parris Island experience though. The pictures don't lie, they just "green" everything. They tint your imagination with Marine-colored lenses and show you all you need to know.

How a person ultimately remembers their Parris Island experience and what they take away from it is up to their DI and the way the individual recruit chooses to handle their experience.

Personally, my recollections are a fond hodge-podge. I've forgotten any dissonance or discomfort. I know I sweated a lot, but I don't remember the sting of it and I know I was tired a lot but I don't recall feeling worn. But I vividly remember the palm leaves whipping each other like bullfighters and the smell of salt and sea and the peculiar balanced sway my walk developed as my feet adapted to the slipperiness of sand underfoot. Even on asphalt, that little three-layer cake was a constant; foot/flesh on top of rubber soles on top of grit. I've had the good fortune to revisit the base in recent years and the island still smells the same, every corner of it, and it takes me right back.

I tell people that on Parris Island you slide through your days. My best friend used to say our time here is short so make the best of it. And always to poetry:

> "Momma and Papa were lying in bed.
> Papa rolled over and this is what he said:
> Uh give me some.
> Uh give me some.
> PT
> PT
> Good for you
> Good for me
> I've been running since the rising sun
> Gonna run all day till the running is done.
> Ho chi min is a son-of-a-bitch
> Got the blue balls, crabs, and the seven-year-itch."

I didn't make it up folks, so don't get mad at me if the language offends you. Raw reality is acceptable and vulgarity is simply a part of the bootcamp and Marine experience. Looking back I remember the word fuck was a noun, adjective, preposition and verb and it was used multiple times in a sentence.

Here's another of my favorite cadences. It's not Dickens but in my book, it makes every day feel like a Carolina Christmas:

"**A** what we gonna do when we get back
Take a shower and hit the rack
NO WAY
Gotta run
PT
A lot of fun
Alo-righty-lao
Alefty-righ-alo
Alo-righty-lao
Left-raighty-lo
Alo-righty-lao
I love to double time
Feels good
Sounds good
Fired up, fired up
Plenty sun
Fired up
Here **we go...**"

Yes, life slides along on Parris Island from reveille to reveille on the heels of its own literature. And you better believe that when that morning trumpet blares, every Marine stands at attention and salutes the nearest US flag or stands at attention showing reverence to the symbol representing the greatest country on earth.

We're not a cultural bunch for sure, but don't disparage us for our narrow aesthetics; we're the ones who fight for your rights to wider freedoms of expression!

Midnight at the Oasis

Back to liberty.

Since a drill instructor's day is usually nineteen or twenty hours long, there isn't much time for recreation. Evenings and weekends don't exist in the traditional sense. So I'll be the first to admit that yes, my extreme schedule contributed to difficulties in my marriage.

Sometimes a new training cycle would begin just a couple of days after the preceding one ended and often even within 24 hours! So, in the course of my two years as a drill instructor, I might have managed to escape the island 30 times. And most of these outings were brief ones—evening excursions usually accompanied by other drill instructors or occasionally by my wife. Truth be told, I was more comfortable with my brothers than my wife.

The jaunts with my DI buddies produced some interesting moments as I, was not the light drinker in the bunch but I held my alcohol well. But for all the balance I brought, it was still like turning bulls loose in a china shop. When you're use to correcting everything that's out of order around you, trying to relax in an atmosphere of carousing "miscreants" who bump into you without apology and spill drinks and wipe the corners of their mouths with their sleeves **is** nearly impossible. It was a good thing we kept to the same places; we were fairly well known by the employees of our haunts, who calmed us down many a time. Awkward moments could have easily have gone south if we'd been in strange surroundings.

And besides, the risk of facing disciplinary actions was huge, so we learned to police our own when many a drill instructor wanted to fight after enough whiskey was poured down his throat. Looking back I am not sure how we escaped some of the bars without arrest. I guess the locals got use to looking past some of our drunken adventures. Most of the cops we encountered in our adventures were former Marines or soldiers from Savannah and they took care of us in more ways than one.

I did get a mild kick watching the sprouts of stupidity displace lucidity in my pals, beer by frothy beer. After all John Daniels and Jack Beem were our closest friends… yes I know I said their names different but when you have known them as long as I have you can call them what you want. Too often the following scenario would play out:

"Hey guys, if we leave now, we can get to the squad bay by 0200 hours and roll the recruits onto the quarter deck and make 'em play midnight twister!"

If they hadn't met a girl, they'd be all for it.

"Alright, put the pedal to the metal…"

Trouble would be averted once more once we made it back to the squad bay for another late night thrashing.

I loved the drive back with the windows down, especially if it was spring or summer, and the relaxed if slurred chitchat of DIs "at ease." The island nights could be mesmerizing and its moon so calming, diced by palm fronds into rippling slices of faded yellow that marched their reflections across the waves at whatever speed we chose.

The moon never beat us to the base but we never outran it either.

I enjoyed going to Plums in Beaufort, wife in tow. In fact, those were probably some of our best moments, enjoying the waterfront from a small table cluttered with appetizer plates and empty shot glasses. If it was a Friday or a Saturday night, a reggae band would aim its music at the patrons and out the huge open window, where it would mingle with laughter and the sounds of shifting chairs and boats far out on the river.

Oysters on the half-shell. Blue fin toro. Man.

I could picture Forrest Gump docking his shrimp boat and yelling for the cooks to buy his haul. They actually filmed part of that movie in the area.

Plums was such an escape, with all its rustic charm and sensory drug feeling, so much like a carnival for the soul that I'd have to shake off it's effects to return my thoughts to whatever was on the next day's agenda. My wife noticed the struggle I think, but never completely understood it. To her, both worlds—the Marine life and the heady rush of our occasional excursions—had elements of fantasy and she just didn't know where to land. She'd figure it all out later, but those were some difficult years for her.

Even the escapes with my wife left me wanting to be with those I would bleed with and sacrifice with. They were a hilarious group of DI's embedded deep in my memory of a great time on Parris Island.

I could see the want in my wife's eyes but at the time I didn't equate "want" with "need."

As for myself, I knew right where to land. The swab of freedom's exhilaration may have soaked me skin-deep, but that's not very deep. I dry off quickly. My boots were more comfortable on Sergeant Death than they were on Mr. McDugle, and I didn't want to blister myself or cripple my stride so I'd repossess my identity with the slightest of mental nudges.

Someday, I'd think, when we have kids I'll swap hats.

The joker in the bunch

One New Year's Eve between cycles, my wife had just hit the rack when the phone rang. It was about 0100 hours, nearly my own rack time. A Beaufort sheriff informed me that his deputies had picked up a buddy of mine, Senior Drill Instructor Staff Sergeant Martin. They had no room in their jail cells, I was told, and besides, he was being belligerent and posed a threat to the other prisoners. Could I come pick him up?

I groaned, annoyed.

"What's he been arrested for?"

"Public intoxication and disturbing the peace."

I could hear SSgt. Martin in the background, "You son of a bitches did not have the right to break up our poker game, I will kick your asses". The sheriff went on and on about the military and its rowdy, stubborn, drunken enlistees and how he didn't have time to babysit for the US government and anyway, he wasn't paid enough and wouldn't care to if he was.

He wasn't paid enough?

I unlatched our door and walked down the steps onto our little patch of grass, stretched the phone cord as I went. I swatted mosquitoes as my discussion with the Beaufort sheriff continued. The whole situation aggravated me and I made up my mind I wasn't going anywhere that night unless an officer ordered me to. And this was below officer radar and needed to stay that way. I didn't buy the sheriff's threats to complain further up—to talk to a general if he had to—because nobody wanted that level of drama.

"Listen," I said, "sounds like he needs to sleep it off. I can't bring him back to the base like that; I will pick him up in the morning after he has had a chance to wake up on the right side."

Suddenly, a bellowing roar crackled the phone's diaphragm, making me jump.

"You sonofabitch, McDugle! You were going to leave me sitting here, weren't you? You sorry fucker, I'm gonna remember this…" I could hear the sheriff and another DI in the background laughing. They'd pulled a prank on me, no one was arrested it was simply a drunken SSGT pulling a 0100 hour prank.

I took heat with laughter for a while from SSgt. Martin for my purported disloyalty. He acted as if I failed the test but I knew that if he were that drunk he needed to sleep it off. After all I would have had to face my wife after bringing home a drunk. Deep inside he knew (they all knew for that matter) that when the real shit hit the fan they could count on me like I counted on them.

The heat

Of all the seasons, summers on Parris Island are the hardest to endure. They don't seem to blow in and blow out as quickly as spring and fall's blustery Atlantic personalities.

The palms and pines that link the swampy marshes trap the sun in and block the sea winds, so the whole base squashes under a hot blanket that can't be kicked off. It's like trying to sleep with a comforter when the air conditioner's not working and its still one hundred degrees outside.

When my cover started to slip sideways on my head bristle and Sgt. Schaffer's nose stayed red, I knew we were in for it. And if the recruit's Marine-issue t-shirts were sagging and sticking to their ribs before PT had even begun, that was a sure sign we'd get the Black-Flag notice.

On a Black Flag day we're not allowed to train or thrash the recruits outside, or at least don't get caught doing it, but there's always the polished cement of the quarter-deck at the head of their squad bays, so they weren't off the hook completely. We'd set them to field daying the squad bay which is something they hated worse than the physical punishments, because we were very inventive and detailed in our methodology and were right at their backs the whole time. Or, march them to a classroom for some mind numbing information reinforcement.

But even moving recruits around from place to place was no fun on a midsummer morning when the sun was ironing the heat back into place before it even had a chance to dissipate. Everything on a military base is connected by asphalt, because marching is the inertia that propels everything en masse and demands an immediate response to commands. So, if the air is one hundred degrees, the ground and the first few feet above it are one hundred and fifteen.

So we'd busy them indoors, and by the end of the day, everybody, recruits and DIs alike, would be doubly grouchy from the time spent in close-quarters. Truth was recruits always stink a bit so I didn't like being jammed in with them. It was miserable for all of us.

"Eyeballs" the Senior DI might say, "Snap Sir" was the reply with every eye in the squad bay looking his direction while he would teach a period of instruction or if he wanted them to continue working he might say "EARS" and their reply would be "Open Sir" as they continued to work but simply shut their pie trap to listen to what he had to say. Some black flag days would be spent cleaning the whiskey locker or in a route step to another location while the platoon would sing"

> "I was born at Parris Island
> The land that God forgot
> The sand was eighteen inches deep
> The sun was blazing hot…"

The ninja

I never came close to feeling sorry for a recruit. Personally, most DI's would hit even harder if that's what it took to a recruit in balance; a few eyes or cheeks would get welted but not as often as the gut.

I had to do that because it was important for recruits to conquer their insecurities and weaknesses and doting our favoring would not reap that result.

Some recruits had a warrior's heart but lacked the equivalent in physical strength or abilities, and they'd try and try, I credit them highly for their fortitude, but just couldn't seem to batter their way to a victory. I'm talking specifically about the more challenging stuff like the boxing ring or a 20-mile hike. It made me want to push them harder and present them with difficult challenges, because I knew if I backed off of them they'd perceive it and would never forgive themselves for not trying harder. The all knew there was no preferential treatment.

I remember a particular recruit, Recruit Puttine. He had all the bravado in the world, but could not break a habit and set himself in the proper Marine fighting stance. He just couldn't do it. He'd contort into some kind of Bruce Lee turtle-crane-tiger thing and start throwing karate kicks.

"What the hell are you doing?" I said the first time I observed his strange pose.

"Sir, this recruit's had a lot of years of karate training and it's hard to break those habits, SIR!"

"So you've had karate training?" I moved closer to him on the sawdust floor of the pavilion and stood between him and his opponent.

"Sir, yes SIR!"

"And you're having a hard time breaking those habits and adopting the Marine methods that have been time and battle proven?"

"Sir, yes SIR!" Beads of sweat freckle his forehead as he stood at attention in the sawdust pavilion.

"Well, I think your years of karate training give you an unfair advantage against a normal recruit, so lemme see if I can match you up better after all I can't let a karate trained recruit kill his opponent. Do I have any Golden-Glove boxers in here?"

A recruit who was actually about the same size as Recruit Puttine raised his hand.

I had them fight each other and recruit Puttine got pummeled. I let the fight continue a little longer than most just to teach this punk a lesson.

"Recruit Puttine," I said, "look at you, son. Your mom and dad threw away all that money on your years of karate training!"

He left the ring a humbled ninja but I have to say, the experience, which might have left others feeling defeated, pushed him to learn and to adapt, rather than throw in the towel, and he eventually became a great fighter, as well as a great Marine.

And he never broke into a ninja stance again.

I saw a lot of recruits along the way that had less going for them than their fellow marines; they were shorter or thinner or uncoordinated or less graced socially. Some had a hard time learning, they just didn't catch on as quick. But I made those guys my job as much as any of the others, and undertook to give them every opportunity to overcome their disadvantages. And ninety-nine percent of the time, they did. Their fortitude of mind developed in time. You can teach skills and knowledge but a recruit has to have heart. Heart is the desire to overcome no matter what you are faced with and no matter how much you lack the skills to achieve it.

I hit the rack that night, chuckling.

Now I'm going to have to humble that Golden-Glove guy, I thought. He thinks he's really something!

Lightning Strikes

Storms on the eastern fringe of our nation are common, especially during the summer. The Atlantic Ocean can churn up some doozies. South Carolinians go on watch at the beginning of every summer and usually need to stay on guard all the way through early winter. Hurricanes, cyclones, thunderstorms you name it, we've experienced it.

Being on an island, our Recruit Training Depot is particularly vulnerable to the first waves of advancing weather. We've never been wiped from the face of the earth—neither Hugo nor Hazel had the power—but the marshes have nearly strangled us at times when they overflowed their saw-grass edges, spilling gators and snakes and leeches into our laps.

Yes, storms can transport chaos, but I've always loved them; they're loud as a rock band and cleansing as a spray of Lysol, washing the pollutions of noise and dust and humidity out of the air so the world can start over fresh once they've passed. I love lightning too, the crack of its splintery whip as it chastises waves far out to sea where they're the most boisterous. There is nothing like being in the middle of the ocean with no land in site and watching a lightning storm rip havoc across the open seas. God must be a cowboy.

Give me a chair a rifle and a good book, and I'll ride out whatever the sky sends, praying it scares up a big buck even a nice doe which would totally take my mind off of the inbound tornado.

Though I have a fondness for the sky's thrashing of the earth (maybe it reminds me of a DI thrashing a recruit in the pit) I carry a spot of sorrow that embitters me sometimes, a memory that drives me to turn something on, a radio or a TV—anything mindless—that will distract me until I quit looking back.

It had been a stormy week and I think we all thought the heavens had drained their power and needed a recharge, so, after checking the weather and making sure everything looked okay, we proceeded to form our platoons for a march down range. It was live fire week and we could not afford to let the storms get us behind our schedule. We'd spent a week dry-firing and classrooms and the recruits were anxious to send rounds down range.

The march out was great, a slight breeze bounced around a scattering of stray clouds like bumper cars in slow motion, the humidity continued show its muggy face but the breeze had a way of making you forget about that. It felt good, our pace was brisk and the recruits were up for anything, pitching a shelter even, if it meant getting out of the squad bays. There are only so many corners one can scrub at with a toothbrush.

When we got to the range, we lined the recruits up and got them busy firing. In small groups, we worked them from the two hundred yard targets to the three hundred and then the five hundred. Only the Marine Corps requires its young men to make a five hundred yard shot in boot camp. It's not an easy thing, but it's do-able. With training, anything becomes easier.

Most of our recruits were still at the two hundred when we received word from headquarters that there was lightening storm in the area. It was just a bruise on the horizon but this is the type of thing you don't take chances with, so we began to form up on the paved road we'd marched in on. Recruits have learned to move fast by now but evidently not quick enough on this day, the storm quickly stretched its black wings out overhead. Literally, it was like day turned into night. It wasn't raining yet, but that wasn't the issue. A good soaking we could handle, but when the hairs on our arms began to stand up, indicating that electricity was saturating the air, we scrambled into emergency mode.

Suddenly there was a bright flash and a loud paper ripping sound and a couple of platoons scattered like roaches in a burned out basement.

We had been in the process of getting the recruits into formation so we could hustle back to the squad bay as each recruit had a rifle on their shoulder. Marine policy is to shut down the range if lightning is within ten miles, but we were too late. Lightning had struck the third squad leader in the top of the head, passing through his body before blowing an eight-inch chunk of pavement from the road beneath him. He was killed instantly.

I couldn't believe it. We were all stunned for a split second, all of us DIs—just in absolute shock—just like the first explosion of combat and the recruits were watching for our reactions. This kid had been well liked and had just taken a third squad leader position. These recruits would find first hand what the fog of war meant and the deep nagging ache of losing the one next to you without a round ever being fired.

Order had to be reestablished, so we reformed our ranks and marched as quickly as we could to the rifle range squad bays, which were located near the tree line. The duty corpsman was on the scene immediately.

Oddly enough, it never did rain and there were no more lightning strikes.

So there you have it, the reason my love for storms is tainted. I still love the power, the wind and the light shows; I'm just pissed off at them for taking the life of one our own.

The DI and the Medic

There is a footnote to that story:

One of the deceased recruit's drill instructor's rode in the back of the ambulance with him as it screeched off to the base hospital. After a few minutes of fruitless efforts, the attending medic gave up on the recruit, which infuriated his drill instructor. No one declares a Marine dead except a qualified medical doctor.

The DI kept telling the medic to work on the recruit, but he was unwilling, given that the guy was unresponsive in every way and had been since he'd been struck.

So, out the back of the ambulance went the medic. The Marines love their Docs but this one gave up too quick. I can say that is an uncommon occurrence, I have never seen anyone sacrifice more than the corpsman attached to the Marines. It is like they have to prove themselves and I have never met a doc that did not live up to that standard until this one incident.

The DI worked on the recruit himself until they arrived at the hospital, where the doctor made him quit and the pronouncement was officially made.

The corpsman should have never quit, but this is also a testament to a drill instructor's loyalty and willingness to self-sacrifice on behalf of the young men he's endeavoring to ready for whatever lay ahead—the real approaching storms, the cracks and pops of a round flying by your grape and grenades busting your eardrums.

For me, that summer ended right there and then. The hot days lingered and smoldered their fuming best, but I had gone on ahead in my mind, determined to ignore the rest of the present season just out of spite for it. My best friend told me there is a great future and hope that is beyond what I could see.

Sergeant Death Looks Back

I was doing the paperwork late one night and began to reminisce. I think it was the unusual quiet that got me thinking. I could see the flags rippling in their spot lit auras just beyond the chow hall and beyond them the tree line of pines that taunted the moon with their spiky tops. The spruces on the base were scattered but beautiful reminders that we weren't floating as far from the mainland as it felt sometimes.

So I rolled back from the desk, nearly knocking the shit can over in the process, and stretched. A stack of papers started to slide off my lap, so I tossed them to a corner of the desk and anchored them with a couple of ballpoints.

My wife would be asleep by now, restless under light covers as our baby pushed and stretched inside of her.

We'd only recently found out, but it was wonderful news. She had been working a civilian job so the extremity of our spectrum needed a focal—a common purpose—to help us tune back into one another. Her pregnancy seemed to be doing the trick.

But where do we go from here? I wondered. It was easy being a Marine and married when all you really cared about was being a Marine. However, I found myself at a new place and I struggled with a love building inside of me for my child and how would that war against me being a Marine? How can I be a daddy too?

I stopped right there. I wasn't good at looking ahead. Too much of my life was spent in the immediacy of what I could see, hear, smell, and detect in the present.

That's when the memory trigger cocked. Everybody's got a history and thinking about my wife brought to mind her smiling young face as she watched me board the bus in Muskogee, Oklahoma that began my Marine Corps adventure. Up to that point, I'd flipped burgers, dabbled as an electrician, and even spent some time at a business college. Nothing had grabbed me. Our beginnings had rambled aimlessly along and my rubbery stabs at real life had fallen so short that I'd begun to battle feelings of unworthiness. Maybe that's why the Marine Corps poster I'd passed by so many times had finally grabbed me.

My dad had served in the army and my granddad had served under General Patton, and I idolized them both. The images and words on the poster seemed to reflect the same message their stories had carried, rifle with themes of honor, so maybe this was destiny's call.

I made a silent vow to the man upstairs; if I pass the ASVAB (an enlistment qualification test) I'll go, and if not, I won't. Then I walked into the recruiter's office and signed up on the spot. I told the recruiter that I was signing up no matter what he told me so he might as well tell me the truth.

My wife was shocked when I walked in that evening and told her I'd joined the Marines. It didn't seem like me. I'd been an average athlete in high school—a church boy who'd never exhibited any sign of leadership ability or exceptional courage.

She asked me if I had joined the reserves or active duty. I told her active duty and she began to cry. It all sank in once I found out I'd passed the ASVAB and that I was going to be a Marine.

Get off my desk!

Seven months later, I was off. My dad and other military men shared their insight, so I prepared the best I knew how. I didn't want to fail at this, I had quit so many other things, so I practiced cadences and marching and exercised and ate to gain weight and did everything I could in my spare time to ready myself for boot camp; I was very intimidated at the thought of not finishing something else I'd started. My best friend told me to not think about the negative but to be positive and to speak confidently about my success to come.

I was as ready as a person could be, but on the bus to the Alfred P. Murrah building in Oklahoma City, I began to question my decision again. My doubts were reinforced when I leaned on a young Marine's desk at the airport to ask a question and he barked, "Get off of my desk!"

His desk? Kevin, you have bitten off more than you can chew, I worried.

Shin Splints

In the end, it all worked out fine. If it hadn't, obviously, I wouldn't be writing this book, but here I am staring at my own story, just as amazed as you, considering how I started.

It didn't all go like I thought. I think my preparations were helpful to some extent, but I over-did it, because no matter how you show up, the process of the Corps is to break you down to dirt and then resurrect you. I'd eaten all that food—probably doubled our monthly grocery bill-and puffed up my frame with strength and muscles that the military apparently saw no immediate need for, in boot camp at least. I went in weighing one hundred and ninety pounds and came out weighing one thirty-five.

Learning my general orders before I went in was a good thing but all that time I had spent in the gym seemed wasted as the corps wanted me to run faster instead of lift more.

Funny, isn't it?

My advice to those preparing to enlist would be this: get ready, work hard at getting into physical shape because it will improve your mental ability and that is more important than anything you can do physically. Go with the attitude that you are clay and you will allow them to mold you into what they want you to become. No matter how prepared you are they will turn you into applesauce anyway. Granted, it is better to be prepared applesauce than puke applesauce, but make sure you are mentally preparing yourself by pushing yourself further and harder than you think you can go.

My experience was like those I've described already; no better or worse or harsher or easier. I had my own Sergeant Death and Sergeant Destruction and Sergeant Satan, only the names we gave them were unprintable.

We had our misfits too.

Private Gregory was a talented computer programmer who'd been awarded a sixty thousand dollar scholarship because of his data dexterity, but he couldn't Marine for beans.

He'd been in boot camp for six months or so—I think he was on his third or fourth cycle—and still hadn't managed to pass certain of the most basic requirements. And I think mentally he was wearing out.

You can tell when someone's giving up on the inside.

As we approached the parade week, and it's demanding marching and drill challenges, frustration in the platoon was heating to a fevered pitch. Being Recruit Gregory's squad leader, it was my responsibility to check his area, check his uniform, make sure he knew where to be and when, and basically babysit the guy. I was actually charged by my drill instructors to make him one of my daily responsibilities. I was quite annoyed at his lack of ability and heart.

One morning before the competitions, my senior drill instructor called me into his house and ordered me to send Recruit Gregory down to medical for a chit stating he wouldn't be able to march with us.

"I don't want that guy on deck because he'll screw up the whole platoon," the SDI bellowed.

"Sir, yes SIR!" I said and went and pulled Recruit Gregory aside and informed him what needed to be done.

"Well, what do I tell them?" he asked.

"Tell them you have shin splints," I said.

"What are shin splints?"

"It means you've got a pain in your shin. Come here. Put your leg up on my footlocker and I'll rap it with my knuckles. That'll give you a pain like shin splints."

He stretched out his leg and leaned back; his arms taught and face pale as he gripped the edge of his rack—as brave as I'd ever seen him.

"Ok, go," he said.

With all the strength I had, I gave my highest knuckle a baseball swing to his shin. I was proud of him—he barely winced, though I knew the injury had probably felt mortal to his broomstick leg.

"But, what if the pain goes away?" he said. I guess he didn't want to feel like he was lying to the nurses.

"Hmm. All right, keep your leg right there." I reached under my rack where I had an extra pair of boots and grabbed one by its top. "Now, hold still."

"Oh, man, no…no!" he said.

Again, I administered a full baseball swing blow to the shin. The heel of that boot sent him jumping down the aisle, grabbing his shin and whooping.

Then, to my astonishment, he came back and put his other leg up, which I gave the same treatment to. This guy is not in his right mind, I thought.

I had to laugh when he came back awhile later with a chit for "cellulites of the feet." The SDI was thrilled, and I felt a weight lift. Our platoon won that day thanks to Recruit Gregory and his brave sacrifice, a deed which was never before **recorded, but** now officially finds itself printed and bound in the annals of Marine love.

Dangerous Girls

After graduating boot camp, I got two weeks of leave.

I spent the time with my family and then returned to infantry training school at Camp Pendleton. On the weekends my buddies and I headed for the beach. California was alluring to a young Okie so I latched on to some adventurous friends and made their plans my own - however wild they seemed.

Thus our drunken haze began. I came in and out of it enough to enjoy the surroundings but a lot of the guys couldn't seem to drink enough—they stayed juiced to the grills.

We'd been warned about the women that peppered the area near the base. They were lock-pickers and zipper-rippers that had their seducing patter down. It wasn't hard to sniff the carnivores from the sheep. There was something formulaic to their flirtations and their hair and makeup seemed impossible to muss. You just knew too much practice had stolen something from their charm and laughter.

A Sergeant Major told me the same girls he'd messed around with fifteen years earlier were still stalking privates the way lawnmowers hunt little green patches that outgrow their yards.

I was newly married and too scared to take a chance while married, yes I was tempted, others with me only narrowly escaped and a few others didn't escape at all but didn't seem to mind being taken advantage of. Those were the ones whose paychecks lasted four or five days, tops. Then they'd be forced to spend the rest of their precious liberty back on the base in a squad bay, eating chow hall food and waiting to ship out to their next training assignment where their loss of dignity would be anesthetized by the routines of training and duty.

Few of us felt sorry for those poor fellows and even fewer of us loaned them our hard-earned money.

"You got a mom, dad or an uncle sam…call them!" I'd say.

Intense Training

Infantry Training School is where a Marine's skills in weapon usage, hand-to-hand combat techniques and other warfare techniques are refined. When you arrive, you're strong, and your confidence has been fed, and you know a little bit...just a little...but not enough to make you dangerous yet. Infantry Training School takes care of that. There, you are turned into a weapon, a force to be reckoned with.

I graduated number one from ITS and was meritoriously promoted, so I got to choose between a couple of interesting options for my next assignment. I chose Bangor, Washington, a nuclear submarine base on the shady, Pacific side of the continental U.S. I figured it would be a nice change from the San Diego heat and maybe I'd get some good fishing in. Not long after I arrived, I was promoted to corporal and made director of the orientation platoon, where I dished out three weeks of intense training to boot camp graduates. They would be responsible for guarding nuclear weapons in a highly restricted area, among other things, so they really had to be on their toes and ready to use deadly force if it came down to it.

Bangor is also where I leaped to the next level, career-wise. My superiors saw something in me that I hadn't, I guess, and urged me to consider becoming a trainer on their Warrior King Team. I accepted and began a thirteen week close quarters battle course—very hardcore—and was one of thirteen that graduated from a starting class of over one-hundred seventy. The intense Marine instructors took us through every close quarter and explosives course imaginable. The FBI academy, CIA training, swat-team training, martial arts training—you name it. Once they had finished all of these courses, these elite instructors wrote a training manual called "The Best of the Best," that included the most efficient tactics and strategies and implementations for close-quarters battle that had ever been developed.

We practiced in abandoned buildings in San Francisco where we entered windows halfway down them, repelling with incredible stealth. We carried an MP5 tactical weapon (a few carried M870 shotguns) that we shot until our fingers were sore from loading rounds, nearly 10,000 a day.

Firing the MP-5 machine gun and transitioning skills were two of my favorite activities from that period. The MP-5 and.45 cal pistol in a well trained hand offered unbelievable stealth and accuracy for close quarter battle!

I believe in God, so I've got to say—I may have been on a military fast track but I think I was also being guided along a more significantly mapped-out and higher intended route as well. The Gulf War kicked off just before all this specialized training ended, so as soon as I had my certificate in hand, I requested to be sent to Saudi Arabia. No way was I going to huddle over more training manuals and try to train others in the deadly arts I'd learned when I could put to use my training in a real combat scenario.

Our shores still looked airbrushed and our innards hadn't been slit open yet, but overseas dark forces were rising and if left unchecked, they would eventually roll over onto us.

So, they said yes. I got my transfer.

My orders were to report to 1st Battalion, 8th Marines, at Camp Lejuene, North Carolina.

It was a week before Christmas, 1990.

It was a long drive from Washington State to Oklahoma, where my wife and parents were, and then on to North Carolina. Forests became grasslands that became mountains that dove down under the plains where they hid beneath scrub oak oasis's that wore names like "Locust Grove" and "Potter's Pond." I was glad there were no babbling co-pilots beside me in my Mazda truck. Sure the time might've gone by quicker but talk wore me out after the solid information had been drained from it. The cassette deck never tired of my tapes though everything from Van Halen to Hank Williams. My mind just needed rhythm to help pace my journey.

The visit with my wife was great, if awkward - and my parents like-wise. They wondered why I wouldn't stay longer. Didn't they give you forty-five days of leave, Kevin?

Yes, but I just gotta go. I gotta.

Off again

When I got back to North Carolina from the 1st Gulf War, I moved my wife from Oklahoma to Camp Lejeune and we signed a year lease on a home. Our bliss, if that's what you could call it, our reuniting was short-lived. Immediately, I received orders to ship out again. I was attached to 1st Battalion 8th Marines and their orders were to show force and help to train allied forces over seas.

We kissed goodbye again, but it felt like a salute, it was becoming such a routine.

She handed me my C-bags and I handed her the keys for another eight-month stint.

Floating

"Floating" is a unique experience. Rather than establish a base, fleet Marines are kept on naval vessels so they can deploy faster. Thus, you float...maybe in the North Atlantic, maybe in the Mediterranean...for six months generally, but sometimes longer.

You get used to the obvious annoyances; the swinging doors and the sliding meal trays and having to brace yourself before you pee sometimes. But you never get used to the exhilaration of empty horizons. I could gaze at the sea for hours and come away with no new thought but feeling like I'd gained something anyway.

Since Marines are the transient ones on a ship, we're given a little space. There was a rack above me and a rack below me. And a small locker in the hallway I could fit a few things into.

I read sixty-five books on that first trip—more than I'd ever read in my life. In fact, I don't think I'd ever finished a book prior to that crossing. And I'm not complaining; the military does its best to keep its troops in training with physical fitness and specialization skills on those long crossings. We'd throw targets off the back of the ship and blow them to bits and practice tactical training maneuvers down the hull. Occasionally we'd port and be granted a liberty in some exotic ancient metropolis.

Sometimes we'd actually deploy, via helicopter, for short missions about which we were given little information. Which was fine—I didn't need to know.

Eventually we neared Saudi Arabia and the only thing I was tired of were the sailors. As a rule we got along, but I think they felt imposed upon and occasionally acted out their resentments with crafty zeal. It is after all their ship until an alarm goes off, at least, and then the Marines own it. That tenuous sense of possessiveness would put anybody on edge, I suppose.

Everybody's got to behave though and generally we did, but not always.

Once, it was discovered that some of the cooks had been making love to loaves of bread then dicing it up for Marines.

Not very hospitable, eh?

They were arrested and, for their own safety, gotten off the ship as quickly as possible. Rumors of men being tossed over the side fill the ship when someone goes missing. It was not common but has happened especially to some arrogant butter bar that thinks his shit doesn't stink. We called them 90 day wonders because they go through Officer

Training in 90 days and then they are put in charge of men with 10, 15 and 20 years experience. The ocean is definitely great at keeping secrets.

Oman came into view and once again I disembarked onto foreign soil.

The heat was about as infernal as heat can be but both the Omani Royal Marines and we bore it with unflinching military perseverance. We taught them what they'd ask to be taught, in their training times not ours. They enjoyed a late start, a long prayer time, soccer and lunch and then they let out early for the day leaving our Marines feeling like we had accomplished little.

I believe some of that sand still inhabits the nooks and crannies of my gear, wherever it is and whoever's using it, because it's one of the finest substances on the earth and just cannot be shaken completely away. It finds its way into everything, like the lizards on the walls of king's palaces in the Bible. It's the thing that gives your mashed potatoes a bit of grit, when all the while you thought it was the course-ground pepper.

It's the spice of the world, that Arabian sand…

Anglico

Time passed. I went back-and-forth once more, traversing the Atlantic with our nation's ornery sailors, and then was asked to try out for ANGLICO, or "Air Naval Gunfire Liaison Company". Being the gung-ho type that thrives on activity, how could I say no?

It's a highly specialized group that consists of no more than five or six hundred personnel worldwide. Its requirements are stringent and you only get one shot at passing. There are no do-overs.

Well, I passed and entered the final phase of my pre-drill instructor career, assigned to 2nd Anglico. Our main job was to support foreign allies and to cross enemy lines and get close enough to put lasers on targets, which close air support, naval gunfire and artillery would then utilize to bring precise, controlled destruction to whatever had been deemed a threat.

I had received my gold Airborne wings by this time. My call sign was Hollywood because I had a number of Hollywood style jumps before joining Anglico. Anglico was known as lightning from the sky and thunder from the sea as we were able to rain down rounds that would suppress and or kill our enemy. Anglico was the unit that usually found itself attached to a foreign ally unit such as the Israeli Seal Team, French Foreign Legion or the Brits. We would provide those allies with all the American firepower they needed.

I enjoyed the next few years immensely. I traveled all over the world and worked with Turks, Brits, Israelis, South Koreans and many others—soldiers from some of the world's bravest and most honorable militaries, and some of the most stupid as well. I won't name names. It is never easy to lose a comrade in combat. Some good men died and bad men died; and that is the life of being in combat. But mostly, the good lived and valor triumphed and the populations of the nations of the earth benefitted from our labors. It's amazing that just a little bit of pressure, call it violence if you must, applied in the right places procures a whole lot of peace for a whole lot of people.

There is no Marine like an Anglico Marine. They are the most physically fit, mentally tough, and funniest pranksters I have ever had the privilege of knowing. I love them. They were of my breed. We shared blood, stories, hardships, and faced death together. Some were married, but even without that responsibility tying them, they would die for their brother. Though we worked primarily with allied forces, we also partnered with Army Rangers, Seals, Special Forces, and other airborne units.

I salute them all.

The Wrong Box

When I got back from my last float with 2nd Anglico, I came to a multi-armed fork on my military path. Every marine faces this juncture at some point. Everybody's got to do what's called a "B" billet (a short-term duty assignment outside the category of their regular job description) if they're going to make a career out of the Corps. Usually, this meant spending some time on embassy duty or as a recruiter, or—as a drill instructor!

So a bunch of us who fell into this category were ordered to attend a meeting where some options would be presented. It was a slightly chaotic affair, with recruiters scampering around trying to solicit candidates for their positions and officers pulling others aside into corner conversations. Everybody had an agenda.

At the entrance to the conference hall, they had sign-in sheets that needed to be filled out and each sheet had two prominent little boxes next to your signature. The text by one box read, " I volunteer to recruit" and the text by the other box read, "I do not volunteer to recruit."

Cringing at the thought of endless hours behind a desk, I drew a big, firm "X" through the box stating "I DO NOT volunteer to be a recruiter" and handed my paper to the attendant, who squared it up with the others in his wire basket.

During the presentation, I heard what I expected to hear. We were told how grand it was to be a recruiter: you get to live off base, eat at restaurants every day, spend the evenings with your wife and help the Corps select its next generation.

I know it sounds like it should've been tempting, but it wasn't. I don't know if I was afraid I'd get fat and lazy or what, but I wasn't ready to settle down yet. Also, the state of my marriage probably contributed to my restlessness. It just wasn't going so well at home. In fact, I felt awkward stepping through the door half the time.

I knew what I wanted to do when I left the meeting but kept it to myself for a while. No sense in getting my wife all riled up. I just got her settled down!

But two months later, I got riled up! Orders came for me to report to a recruiting office in San Diego.

What the hell, I thought?

Pissed off and ready to fight the General if I had too, I scooped up the order and its little white envelope and marched off to my Sergeant Major's office.

"SGT Major," I said, "this is bullshit. I want to be a drill instructor, not a pussy recruiter. In fact, I am not made sit behind a desk!"

He shifted in his chair and took a sip of coffee from his ANGLICO mug. His eyes were scanning me for determination. He wanted to make sure I meant what I said.

"Alright, McDugle, call your Monitor in Virginia and ask him what happened and see if he can make the switch from recruiter to DI."

Every Marine has a Monitor, which is the equivalent of a career counselor. He plays a behind-the-scenes roll in a marine's assignments and opportunities, though the two may never meet in person.

Sometimes they never even speak.

Mine was about to have a conversation he'd never forget.

Freakin Pogue

I called him that very afternoon and choked back some choice and pre-chosen expletives as I explained to him the problem. I wanted to present my arguments pressed, starched, and in tight formation so this "man of power" wouldn't immediately dispatch me to Never-Never Land. I might get one conversation with this busy pencil pushing pogue.

After a minute of small talk, I got straight to the point and told him about the orders I'd received.

"Let me ask you this, Sergeant McDugle," he responded. "What box did you check on your sign-in sheet at the Billet Conference? Do you remember those two little boxes at the bottom?"

"Yes, I remember them," I said, "and I checked the one that said 'I do NOT volunteer to recruit.'"

"Well, there's the problem," he laughed. "Those that checked the do not volunteer box are the first ones I gave orders to" In my mind I pictured him bouncing his fat ass gut as he laughed until he was nearly out of breath.

"So, Sergeant McDugle," he continued, "…It looks like you will be recruiting America's finest, and I deny your wish for a change of orders…."

I was quick to end our phone conversation. That Mother Fucker, I thought, fuming. Talking to that shitbird didn't get me anywhere. The next morning I revisited the Sergeant Major.

When I told him what the Monitor said I saw his pupils narrow until they looked like artillery rounds in a barrel. He grabbed his phone and scratched at a scarred tattoo on one arm (it looked like an old burn) while he waited for the other party to pick up. When he'd gotten the 2MEF SGT Major on the line, he told him the story and apparently it pissed him off too. The speakerphone was on so I could hear his response:

"Alright, dammit, I've had about enough of this monitors shit. This is the twentieth time I've heard complaints about him. They have no business making career decisions for combat marines from behind their shiny desks.

"I want two things by Monday morning. One, I want orders for McDugle to go to the drill field, and two…I want retirement papers on my desk. Damn bureaucratic imbeciles. Make sure all the 'i's' are dotted and all the 't's' crossed on my paperwork so all I gotta do is sign on the line.

"And one more thing…

"Yes, Sergeant Major?

"You make sure that fucking pogue of a master sergeant gets sent overseas." "Will do."

Click. And that was that. Everything came into alignment—pressed, starched, and in tight formation. The domino line fell where it needed to fall and stood where it needed to stand.

Monday morning, everybody had their orders; the Sergeant Major, the monitor in Virginia and myself. Once again, the efficiency of the Marine Corps proved itself when push came to shove. The pushed may have been within our own ranks, but I believe with all my heart everybody ended up right where they needed to be. The Sergeant Major's wife was thankful, I'm sure.

Basic Training Again

A gust of sea wind howled up a loose drainpipe outside the hatch, rattling it against the DI house. I threw down the ink stick I'd been gnawing on and grabbed another cup of coffee. I was glad no one else was around. I had not looked back at the past in a long time and it was helping to revitalize my perspective. Soon, I'd make the night's last walk through the squad bay - but I was thinking about leaving the recruits alone tonight. If they were all at attention in their racks I wouldn't disturb their bone weary unconsciousness. I had been one of them, after all—not once, but twice—so I knew a complete rest at least one day out of five was essential.

When my DI orders came in '03, I had a weird, double-minded moment. On the one hand, I was getting my wish and had thirty days to collect my things and my wife and get us to Parris Island, South Carolina. I was going to be a drill instructor! On the other hand, I had this gut feeling that repeating boot camp as a seasoned marine was going to be psychologically challenging. We would be stripped down and yelled at once again, and I wasn't sure how I'd react to that after years in the field.

I landed in a company with two hundred other DI wannabe's, and I remember the first morning quite well. Nobody looked out of place but every smile was halved by tension and well wishes were terse and unconvincing. We were grown men about to be called "boys" again - and shits and turds. And so it went.

We were formed up and then introduced to our drill instructors that proceeded to cuss us as they ripped our chevrons off and thrashed us like new recruits. This time it was happening to seasoned combat marines who could not be broken.

It was just like I'd remembered it, with the addition of a torture I'd never even conceived could exist. Sand fleas. As if the mosquitoes weren't enough, God had created a little hard-shelled demon that loved flesh but was content to rest between meals in the ground-up seashells in our little paradise. They're patient tormentors who arouse at the slightest vibration and swarm indiscriminately up the nearest sweat-slicked surface.

You never get used to them. You just don't. You close your eyes and imagine you're an alligator refreshing in cool mud while they nibble up into your shorts and the back of your neck as your DI counts your push-ups; "...ninety-eight, ninety-nine, one hundred..."

You leap to attention but they're still there and you can't move to brush them off or you'll find yourself getting choked within a second of your life.

Parris Island…the land that God did NOT forget. No, he knew the Marines would land there someday and that every proud man needs a thorn in his side!

There's a big difference between boot camp and drill instructor school: In DI School we get to go home at the end of the day. 1700 was usually quitting time (although we were up half the night memorizing drill movements). Our class was different. We didn't need to re-learn how to take apart and reassemble a rifle or have to memorize Marine history all over again. Instead, much of our time was spent learning how to teach others how to dress, how to stand, how to salute and how to drill, etc…

There is a script for every drill movement taught to recruits and drill instructors must be able to repeat them verbatim, word for word.

For instance, what follows is the 1st period of instruction, which dictates how a drill instructor will inform his recruits regarding standing at the position of attention. This is one of the first things a recruit will hear from his new DI and through the ages it has always been announced loudly as his petrified platoon watches, white knuckling their knees:

"Sit up straight and get your eyeballs on me. I said sit up straight and get your eyeballs on me. Notice how the drill instructor's feet are at a 45 degree angle. His heels are on line and touching, his legs are straight but not stiff at the knees, his hips and shoulders are level and his arms hang naturally to the side. His thumb is along his trouser seam and his fingers are in a natural curl. His chest is lifted and his chin is tucked in slightly. Notice when I walk in front of the drill instructor his head and eyes remain to the front. Most importantly his mouth is shut. I say again, his mouth is shut! While aboard Marine Corps Recruit Depot, Parris Island, South Carolina, you will address all personnel, Navy, Marines and civilians at the position of attention."

There are 27 of these drill movements to be memorized and, although this one is short, seven of them are six pages long each. We would be tested on all of them.

But other than these instructional differences–boot camp was boot camp.

We were boxed, sticked, bullied through the Confidences Courses, jibed and tortured. The instructors at DI school were the best of the best. First Sergeant Word was one of the toughest. He was a seasoned vet who had eyes in the back of his head.

Oh, I recall the agonies...
"McDugle! CURL YOUR FINGERS!"
"I'll take all of your butts to the pit!!!"

We had two-man rooms, which was another luxury they didn't offer to new recruits. Nothing fancy, though. I had a small sink that stuck its lip out from the wall next to the head and to walk from there to my rack took three steps. Two wall lockers braced up the corner of the room. And that was it.

My roommate and I had a crockpot and we'd make rice and sausage if we weren't venturing off the base, which was infrequent. We were always studying, studying, studying...

The single guys made little breaks for the women's DI side but very little came from those forays; the women drill instructors were as sharp and watchful as the men and had no tolerance for frivolity. There were rules about that kind of stuff anyway and nobody really wanted to jeopardize their careers over fun and games.

The ninety days went by pretty quickly, overall. I had no trouble with any of it. In fact, I guess I did all right, which would result in my being sent to that first lame platoon I described in chapter one.

I saw an old lady walkin' down the street.
She had a pack on her back, boots on her feet.
I said, "Hey Old Lady, where you goin' to?"

She said, "I'm going to Drill Instructor School."
I said, "I'm goin' to Drill Instructor School."
I said, "Hey, Old Lady, I think you're too old;
You'd better leave that stuff to the brave and the bold." She said, "Listen, Sonny, I'm talking to you;
I'm an instructor at the Drill Instructor School.

One Last Check

I smiled as I recalled that old cadence, and poured my fourth cup of "night watch." The clock said 0200 so I figured I better make my rounds. Passing between the silhouettes of the barracks, I was reminded of the low buildings in Kuwait's outskirts and how the nights here sometimes felt like the nights **there—stifling** but velvety, exotic but standard.

I leaned on the rail of the ladder well outside the squad bay and lowered my cover brim. That fourth cup had jazzed me and now I was re-thinking my plan to go **easy** on the recruits. I looked up past some jet trails as far into the indigo as I could and whispered, "What would you do?"

Like any good Marine DI, I took a breath, listening, and then walked through the hatch.

"Who was snoring?" I hollered. "I heard some little Benedict Arnold snoring, what are you trying to give away our position? You CAN'T SNORE WHEN YOU'RE AT ATTENTION!"

How to Make a Recruit Pee
(and other stories)

"I used to sit at home all day
Watching my life just waste away
Then one day a man in blue
Said, "Son, I've got a job for you"
Trouble and adventure and loads of fun
We'll even teach ya how to shoot a gun
So I signed the papers and I got on the plane
I went to the place where they made Marines
Parris Island was the name of the place
First thing I saw was a drill instructor's face
He had razor creases and a smoky bear
There were mountain-climbing privates everywhere Singing, "Low righta le-eft…ah left righta le-eft…"

I loved to double-time my recruits with this one; it was one of my favorite marine cadences. We'd be out marching some path near the fringes of gator territory where the marsh grass danced in gusty circles and I'd make sure nature knew who was in charge of this world. Or this patch of it, anyway! Marine Corps drill instructors!

By 1994, I'd topped the record I'd mentioned previously. In between cycles that spring, I'd done my duty as a DI and actually hollered loud enough to cause the bladder muscles to loosen from seven fresh-faced recruits. I was trying to get a whole row to let go, but springs that trickled forth were random among the ranks. I knew the Ohio gangster was going to be one of them. For all his posing and bravado (which would ultimately see him through marvelously) he's spent too much time without rules or role models. He's probably spent too much time in the back alleys of Cincinnati in the shadows of the night.

I was too much, too soon, and too loud.

Few noticed but the drill instructors because everybody else is face front and trembling, not even daring glance even at their own noses. I don't say this in arrogance but in reality.

There's no shame in it if they could weather the teasing about it and forget it and move forward. They'd often make some of the best Marines the Corps turned out. If they could not, peeing your pants and crying was a boy's way of exiting, leaving room for a man to take your place.

And that Ohio fellow—it didn't surprise me he let loose either. Some of the biggest guys have the least control over their functions because their brains are too far away from those parts of their bodies. That's my logic, at least, although I know there's no science to back it up.

And just as a side note, because I've been asked—no, nobody ever shit their drawers. If they had, that would've taken some guts to live down and temporarily earned them a position ten paces behind the rest with their rifle over head just like the pee bodies, and a night sleeping in the head. I said head (toilet) not grape.

The only shit story I could tell would be an incident of my own devising. I would've made the producers of "Punked" proud with my ingenious plot.

The gross-out

I'd threatened my squad leaders during a certain squad bay inspection, so they had the recruits spend the better part of an afternoon detailing their squad bay. Sergeant Shaffer and I were there the whole time—we wouldn't leave them to themselves when the stakes were this high) I think the Battalion Commander was going to be passing through) so we were hovering over them and up their butt-cracks the whole time. Breathing hot coffee and garlic breath down their necks.

Finally, after hours of microscopic disinfecting, I called the guide and squad leaders aside my house and told them to prepare for inspection.

Now, I'd been hatching my master plot for some time; I'd thought of it one day as some of the other DIs and I pined about our favorite childhood soft drinks and candy bars. Something just went click in my mind and I made a big mental note on the ornery side of my brain.

Checking the personal areas between their racks, I ranted and raved and pawed at the slightest discrepancies, watching for despair as I jarred loose something they'd spent time lining up just perfectly. I pointed to a clean porthole and smeared my finger on its glass to check for dust, leaving a smudgy print that Sergeant Schaffer, who was following behind me, would give them hell for.

Slowly, I made my way toward the head. That was the place we'd usually nail them good so they tensed as we started scrutinizing the sinks and the mirrors and the deck, saving the urinals and stools for last. Leaning into one of the stalls, I remarked to the four squad leaders, "You know you're going to pay dearly if I find one spot on my shitter…"

I got on my hands and knees to examine the inside of the shitter, and that's when I pulled out my finger with a previously melted swipe through a Snickers bar. I'd melted it slightly in the microwave and kept it hidden in the curl of my fingers until the inspection. Its room temperature, chunky, greasiness had coalesced perfectly.

I let out a howl as I pretended to dig under the bowl beneath the seat with my fingers.

"Oh hell," I hollered. "Is this shit?"

I waved the sticky brown goo at them then brought it to my nose, taking a big sniff. "It smells like shit," I said. I put my chocolate covered finger in my mouth. "It tastes like shit. It is shit!"

The squad leaders were ready to freaking die. Did our drill instructor just eat shit? The rest of the platoon could hear my tirade out in the squad bay.

"Sergeant Schaffer," I said, "do you want to double check this."

"Naw, that's okay," he said. "I believe ya." He turned to the squad leaders. "All right, you nasty fucks, we're going to start all over again, from the beginning! GET MY FREAKIN' HEAD CLEAN!"

I pounded down the aisle between them with my best growling bear face on, licking my lips clean, wondering if anybody would retch.

What a perfect exit. Not a word needed to be said. I had laid wonder and confusion in the eyes of the recruits, perception is reality, who is this shit eating DI anyway? Shaffer later laughed, "Did you see the look on their faces?"

Drugs on deck

In the last thirty days or so of a training cycle, drill instructors are given a seven-day break. It's called Mess Week. One DI stays on duty and the rest get some down time. The recruits are farmed out to different assignments and kept busy. Some go to the chow hall. Some are assigned to maintenance or mowing crews. Others are sent to the field. Whatever they end up doing, it flows from the previous week's activities so they take it as just another stage of boot camp.

During one of these respites, it was my turn to be the one duty DI and keep an eye on the squad bay, which was relatively empty during the day, and keep up the administrative bullshit. Do the paperwork, in other words.

Well I had just arrived and gotten settled behind my desk one crisp morning—it was Wednesday, I believe—when a series of loud raps at the hatch broke the wonderful silence.

Then, "Sir, Recruit Morgan requests permission to speak, SIR!"

"Go away," I said.

Three more loud raps (the knocker was following protocol perfectly) shook the red board attached to the bulkhead. It had a yellow handprint painted on it. "SIR, RECRUIT MORGAN REQUESTS PERMISSION TO SPEAK, SIR!"

"I SAID GO AWAY, RECRUIT!" I was getting aggravated. A recruit should never persist if a drill instructor has said no about something.

"But it's an emergency, SIR!"

"What kind of emergency?" I asked.

"Sir, Recruit Danoka just swallowed a whole bottle of pills, sir!"

Oh, great. I grabbed my cover and followed Recruit Morgan to the squad bay. Recruit Danoka was leaning drowsily against the bulkhead, one arm propped on his footlocker and the other swinging off the edge like a clock pendulum. Sure enough, an empty pill bottle lay beside him. It was Marine issue, so apparently he had a condition of some kind, but that didn't make any difference right now.

"Get to your feet recruit! Did you swallow that whole bottle of pills?" I asked Recruit Danoka.

"Sir, yes SIRRRR-ah!"

"Well, get your canteen and guzzle it. That'll wash the pills down and make 'em kill you a little quicker, you got that!"

I stomped away, leaving Recruit Morgan standing there with his loaded buddy, who looked puzzled, and high. I'm sure they wondered why I'd leave a dying excuse for a man, but I believed it was always important to make a point of being intolerant before letting a threat force me to do something I didn't want to do.

Of course, I marched back to my house and called the medics promptly. They took him to medical and flushed his gut with some god-awful powder that induces puking and then put him on suicide watch where he spent a day in recovery.

I've mentioned before how difficult it is to get out of the Marines and this case proved to be no exception. Danoka was removed from our platoon and reassigned where he could be watched more carefully. He was also given corporal punishments and humbler duties to keep him busy while he went through a series of psychological evaluations. He was eventually outed for "suicidal tendencies" but it took him months to go through the process. He could've been a full-fledged Marine by then!

Recruit Morgan recovered from his shock just fine. I believe he was glad when that week was over and the other recruits were back around to absorb some of Sergeant Death's attention. I was too.

One of the Boys

I never hit a recruit that did not deserve it. I never felt intimidated by a new recruit, no matter his size. And we got some big ones. Alabama and the Carolinas, along with some of the bread basket states, seemed to churn out some American giants. Corn and jambalaya fed boys. But big on the outside doesn't always mean big on the inside and even if it did, there were usually three or four other DI's around so the match would never be even. I think the bigger fellows came in knowing they might be targeted though, and tried to keep low profiles.

And though we had some smart asses, I never witnessed a recruit threaten a drill instructor.

Sometimes for fun, I never knew it to be for any other reason, a large drill instructor would be planted in a platoon as a guinea pig. He'd show up with the recruits in the very beginning, standing on the yellow lines with them, acting like he'd just shipped in from Hayseed Pasture, Wisconsin. He might get lippy with the processing DIs, just to set a tone, then once they moved to their new squad bay, the training officially started.

Then the fun would begin.

At some point, the imposter would take a stand against he smallest DI on the team when everybody else was around, so all eyes would be on them. He might refuse a command or yell obscenities—just be shockingly rebellious in general—to the little DIs feigned chagrin.

Then the little DI would knock the shit out of him with one blow.

'Nuff said!

You'd better believe they'd never have a problem with that platoon!

I had a little game of my own that was similar to this.

I called it, "One-of-the-boys."

Very few of the other platoons were made to sleep in the position of "attention" as I made mine do. I'll reiterate my reasons: it teaches them that comfort is not a requirement and keeps them in a state of readiness. It's okay to be uncomfortable but it's never okay to be unprepared.

So I'd get bored on some of those night shifts and go for walks. And it was on one of those gamboling strolls, as the moon clamored hopelessly for my mind's attention, that I hatched my newest plan. It was shrewd and perfect and one I could try out immediately.

I headed back to the DI house, took off my DI cover and slipped on my PT gear so I was dressed like my recruits. Then I walked back into the squad bay and slid between the racks until I'd found one issuing the resonance of muffled conversations. At 2 am, everyone should be asleep but some recruits apparently had a clandestine gathering going on. And I was really, really interested in joining the conversation. Or, at least, I was interested in causing some trouble!

I approached them quietly—they didn't even know I was there.

They were showing each other personal family pictures and laughing, and only glanced at me briefly before returning to their conversation. I was just another recruit as far as they knew. They were engrossed in their glossies, I guess.

I reached them and looked over the shoulder of one, who whipped around like I'd gotten too close and started to open his mouth to tell me off. I spoke first though with a hand to the throat as I threw him to the ground.

"Do you recruits know what time it is? While you are talking about Jody Rotten Crotch the enemy will take you out because you are undisciplined!!"

The gravel in my voice confirmed what had begun to register already—that I was not an older recruit with a picture or two of my own to share.

What followed was quite an event, maybe the first in marine history, but I doubt it: quiet thrashing. I didn't care if I woke up the rest of the world, but as to not draw attention from outside the squad bay I demanded absolute silence as I tore them up on the quarterdeck, in the head and back to the quarterdeck. I guess they learned their lesson because the rest of the night was eerily quite as they all laid at attention letting the sweat run down their face onto the crisp pillow and blankets below them.

Secret Visit

One thing I learned early on was to never leave your recruits alone when other drill instructors are nearby. It's not a good idea, even for a minute or two. DI's seem to enjoy harassing one another's platoons, and I'm not exempt from such time-passing pleasures.

I walked into Senior Drill Instructor Sergeant Channell's squad bay one muggy night, just to say hello, and to my amazement, found that nobody was home except his dapper third-phase recruits. Neither he nor his junior DIs were anywhere in sight.

The bay looked so squared away—it was in such tip-top shape—that it bothered me. Like a designer, I had a built-in corrector that liked to nudge the corner of a painting just a fraction even if it was hanging square. I enjoyed putting my hands on things, just so I could say they'd been there!

I strode the aisle between their racks, impressed by the shine of their immaculately polished boots and the overall order of the squad bay. Rifle hanging on the rack, cable through the ejection port and lock on zero. His recruits knew me by sight, of course, but had not had any interaction with me, so they were apprehensive, and rightfully so.

I had a little drill, which I commanded them to execute.

"Two sheets and a pillowcase, and get on line now!"

Five minutes later I left, ordering them to remain in their positions until their drill instructors returned.

When Senior Drill Instructor Sergeant Channell returned, he would find his recruits lined up in their skivvy drawers, mattresses under their left arm, their pillowcases and blankets piled on the floor. The contents of their footlockers were strewn all the way up the middle of the bay. Their boots were tied in one big ball on the quarterdeck. It would take an hour or two to return the tidy platoon to their former glory.

The next day, Senior Drill Instructor Sergeant Channell approached me on the parade deck.

"McDugle, did you pay a visit to my platoon last night?"

His scarred face and narrow ride of a nose cut a much-needed line between his close-set eyes, which glared at me with a humorous twinkle.

"Why the hell would I visit your nasty platoon?" I said with a light grin.

He stared at me, hands on his hips.

"Well, somebody tore up my platoon last night and they said it was a DI with gold wings on his uniform. And they said he had blue eyes."

"My eyes actually have more of a greenish hue," I said. "Maybe it was Harrigan."

"Yeah, right," he said. "McDugle, if I find out it was you, I'm going to send my juniors over when your recruits aren't looking and have them terrorize those chubby pigs of yours."

"Chubby? Who's chubby?"

He laughed. "I've seen McNabb, your baby-faced jello bowl. Better cut his meals back a little more. Or better yet, just let me have him for a couple days. I'll let the sand fleas chew his hide in my 'special' pit. The one out behind the 'Two Marshes' run."

"Naw, we'll be all right Sergeant Channell. His face looks fat, but that's just his genes. The rest of him is cut like all my other guys." I started away, then turned. "You got a special pit?"

"I'll show ya sometime," he laughed as he strutted away.

It had all been in fun and was received that way. I'd pay for it somewhere down the line, but for now, I played it like I'd been taught; deny, then counter accuse.

Catching up to my platoon as they marched toward the chow hall, I caught myself wondering about Senior Drill Instructor Sergeant Channell's special pit. Was he for real? I determined to take a walk out by the Two Marshes trail next time I had the opportunity.

Might be something I could booby-trap.

The island had a good supply of thorn bushes. Their little spiky orbs, when buried like mines, would make a pit thrashing difficult to endure.

Then again, I could plant cow manure in the sand…

Sadly, Sergeant Channell was killed a few years later in Saudi Arabia. I miss him, he was a great Marine. I pray for his wife and daughter every time I think of him. He was a Marine of Marines and one of the best.

The flying cover trick

I'm pretty sure my DI character (and yes, by that I mean my ornery demeanor) developed in part as a result of surrounding influences. The roster of top-notch DIs I worked with was infamously noted for its impish personalities. And these, no doubt, were simply practicing the traditions of their predecessors—giants of boot camp lore whose bellows, in actuality, were I'm sure the most genuine and life loving of men anywhere. Stress and humor together form the correctly knotted shoelace.

Drill Instructor Sergeant Flannery, aka Sergeant "Satan", made me laugh more than most. And oftentimes his funny performances seemed like movie outtakes—things that could only happen once in eternity because too many of the details had to be engineered at the exact, proper moments. Regardless of what most may think, DI's do not go through some comedian school before they become a hat.

One night, we were getting the recruits ready for their racks, going through the BDR Basic Daily Routine of cleaning and boot shining and organization—straight by the numbers—and finally it came time for lights-out.

Six platoons in six different squad bays were getting ready to hit the rack, so this meant six different set of lights had to be turned off at the exact same time.

Our procedure for this was to have six recruits assigned specifically to the test standing ready outside, waiting for the signal. One of them would be in charge of counting down the time so that all the switches could be flipped simultaneously.

The light recruit in this case was a Pilipino kid—I don't remember his name—but I'm sure he had a hard time understanding English. Before the duty recruit yelled "lights out," the room went dark, a good fifteen or twenty seconds earlier than Sergeant Flannery expected.

Suddenly, in the momentary gloom, I heard an explosive "oof!" then a gasping for air.

When the lights came back on, Sergeant Flannery was missing his cover and the Pilipino recruit was doubled over. Flannery had thrown his rigid DI cover like a Frisbee and nailed the kid right in the gut. It made me wonder if he'd spent a lot of time practicing his aim, because there'd been a good thirty feet between him and his target.

Holly shit, I thought, gritting my teeth against the laughter I had to suppress in good conscience. I had never seen an expression like the one the young recruit was wearing. The color was returning to his face and his breathing was leveling out, but his eyes remained bewildered and his texture was waxen as the DI cover spun like a dying quarter on the deck in front of him slowly waffling to the floor.

To everybody's chagrin, especially Sgt. Satan's, the process had to be repeated all over again but it went off with military precision the second time.

"Fi..."

"For..."

"Three...two...wan..."

No "oof" this time.

Shower Hi-jinx

We were laughing about the incident the next day as we marched our platoon to morning chow. FYI, no recruit ever saw any of us smile or laugh.

"You ever done that before?" I asked Sergeant Flannery.

"Yup!" he giggled. "But my aim has never been that good. Honestly, I was ticked and just threw my cover out of frustration, hoping it would hit something and get his attention. When I heard it hit him, I was surprised myself!"

"I'm gonna remember that one," I said, a little distracted.

For some reason, the platoon seemed slouchy—kind of ambling and inattentive, and a few hadn't responded as quickly as I liked that morning. My jaw was starting to clench and I felt like I needed to release some tension.

"Think I'm going to run these boys," I said.

"All right then," Sergeant Flannery replied. "I've gotta stop by the Senior's office, so I'll see you after chow,"

"See you in fifteen," I said. "And show the Senior your cover trick. Well, on second thought, keep that one to yourself. He might try it on us!" He grinned and headed off toward a row of buildings east of us.

I shouted to the recruits, "Cover down, align, double-time, MARCH!" Normally, you're supposed to walk recruits for thirty minutes before chow so this was not exactly according to Marine regulations, but they were pissing me off.

When we finally got to the chow hall, I only gave them two minutes to eat, then ran them directly back to the squad bay. They were still acting like first phase recruits for some reason. Sometimes, toward the end, recruits will slack up a bit, especially if they've done well during the competitions, and these guys were showing signs of that very type of attrition.

As Flannery would put it, "air bubbles were forming in their maggot-brains."

Well, I still had a few tricks up my sleeve that I saved for near graduates and maybe today was the day to whip them out. Treat an experienced platoon like its the first day of boot camp and it sends them into flash-back shock. Makes their eyes roll up in the backs of their heads.

"Grab your gasmasks," I ordered.

They scrambled, recognizing the intensity of my command.

Then, "GAS, GAS, GAS…" With this command, they quickly donned their gasmasks. They were well trained and had been through the gas chamber experience already.

"Get in the head, RIGHT NOW."

The shower area was pretty large, but it was still crowded, with seventy or so recruits cramming it from wall to sterile wall. They still had their field uniforms on, so they were starting to cook—I could see trickles of sweat beading around the seams of their gas masks. It was about to get even warmer.

One by one, I opened the "hot" handles all the way, until every showerhead was jetting out steamy water. Then we began our physical training.

"Side-straddle hops," I ordered, "and be silent." I didn't want to alert anybody to our activity.

Steam and sweat became one in that room. Their gasp for air through their gas mask was evident.

"Push-ups," I ordered, "sit-ups, side-straddle hops." They looked like flopping seals on a beachfront. Exercise is tough, but add the gasmasks and very little air gets through, increasing the intensity. We used to train this way to get used to higher altitudes, so it wasn't something I hadn't done myself.

"Sit-ups."

I worked the snot out of them, literally. Back and forth we went, from one routine to another, non-stop. Their hands clawed frantically at the tiled floor for traction, but to no avail; they were sliding into each other and careening this way and that. The side-straddle hops had to be miserable, as elbows bashed ribs and chins—not to mention the weight their sweat drenched uniforms and gear added to them, making every moment an agony.

I could see anger behind a few of the foggy lenses, signaling a residue of rebellion, but that was a condition that could be remedied. I'd mark those guys as needing additional attention. A slow response to orders is not an option so this was a lesson well deserved.

I'd positioned a junior DI at the door—one of our new guys—and his eyes were wide with disbelief and fear of being caught as I dished out the devising of the bottom drawer of my training toolbox. Sergeant Brown was his name—a newbie DI who could not march his way out of a wet paper bag. I wasn't entirely sure if I could trust him.

But, for whatever reason, that morning he was alert and I was glad, because I knew that Gunnery Sergeant monitors (we called them the secret police) had been seen prowling the base that day, and what I was doing was pretty extreme when you consider their bellies were full of chow. A report by the monitors of my unorthodox methods would not sit well with the officers in charge of the base's public profile and reputation. It could end my career.

Suddenly, Sergeant Brown jerked and mouthed, pointing a finger, "monitor…!"

Doggone it. One was headed down the catwalk.

Quick as I could, I got the recruits up and out of the head and turned the showers off. As they poured back into the squad bay, I was screaming at them, "You better have those gas masks cleaned and wiped off and in your left hands as you leave this head…"

A sorrier bunch I've never seen, but they hustled.

As they formed on line in the squad bay, I intersected the Gunnery Sergeant and began a conversation with him:

"Good morning, Gunny."

"Good morning," he said. Why are the boys so sweaty? Chow was only fifteen minutes ago.

"Yeah, well, we're steaming out our gas masks, Gunny. Getting the field dust off 'em."

"Sure you were," he said, turning back up the catwalk. "Take care of yourself, Mac."

"You too, Gunny…"

Boy, was I glad my name never had, and never would, find its place on a line on his little brown clipboard.

In the end, all of the torments and challenges of boot camp form a total experience that is unique to each cycle and each individual recruit. He or she will take away an account that will be shared with family members and friends for years to come. What seemed harsh at the time will be looked back upon fondly, and a drill instructor's chastisements will be recited word for word, and every punishment recollected with brave laughter.

The McDugle's

Our trailer at Parris Island was unique in that it was located on the swampy side of the island. Only a fence separated our backyard from the alligators. Sounds like hillbilly living Duck Dynasty style, doesn't it? It was beautiful actually, one of those environments whose glory is in the details; everything was green and growing and sparkled with a light made mysterious as it passed through the island's dense condensation.

The very air was filled with color and the heat of the day burst its hot popcorn-like particles, releasing a fragrant tang that became more pungent—more powerful—as evening approached. I marveled how you could close your eyes and sense the creek and its frothy stirrings. It pressed its muddy banks under which catfish staked out rooty crevices while ripples marked the trail of perch that had scolded nosy gators with their tails. I would point out the large, moss-covered Sycamore to my wife and we'd watch turtles line up on the cracked skin of its lower most branch which divided the creek's surface like a bridge.

We had a little brown picnic table outside; one leg was half an inch shorter than the others so it rocked when we leaned on it. We enjoyed some quiet moments there, swatting mosquitoes from each other's shoulders and flies from the potato salad.

A rum and coke went down smoother when dusk was wrapping the woods and the realities of our everyday lives were pushed towards the ocean side of the island—the busy, structured side. When the sun went down and our windows cast the glow of their sixty-watt strength into the swamp's emerging shadows, our trailer seemed like it belonged there as much as any stump. We felt we belonged there, pressed together by the smell of tropical isolation, a sensation that helped the graceful limp of our strained relationship along a little further.

We didn't have to glance far to break the spell. Our trailer was connected to the next which was connected to the next by the crucified and sagging power lines that rooted us all to the mother ship, keeping us dependent on a world that seemed so distant at times. All of these trailers were where Marine Drill Instructors would catch a few hours of sleep if they were lucky enough to go home that night.

There were other relics of reality too.

Except for deep in the latest hours, the drone of cadence was ever-present, like an electric buzz or the ratcheting of a distant cicada swarm, always there to remind us that paradise was only in our minds. But what was paradise to me? I loved the sound of cadence and the thump of heels from a third phase platoon hitting the deck. It was a nice reminder for me, though, much as I loved the momentary illusions. One that helped me feel comfortable in my own skin.

My wife hated it. I swear she developed second eyelids like a cat's and had learned to close them against all that poked against her hopes and dreams.

Manso

As if to underscore her sensitivities, a tragedy occurred that would shake the whole base awake.

It was after midnight one sultry evening and I'd just walked in the door to find her leaning against the kitchen counter with a glass of sun tea. Usually she'd be sound asleep, so I was surprised and even annoyed a bit that my routine was being tampered with. But I had a feeling why she appeared so fragile and shaken. Her fingernails chattered on the cheap glass as she dabbed at a few streaks of tears with a tissue.

"Oh my gosh, did you hear what happened today?" she said. "Is it really true?"

I leaned against the opposite counter and grabbed a damp rag to wipe dark swaths of island dust from my arm. "Yes," I answered, my Marine heart breaking. "If you're talking about Manso (I have changed the name out of respect for his family), yes it is."

"Oh Lord," she sniffed, clutching her glass as though there was nothing else solid in the universe. "How is Sue?"

"Well, you know she was going to divorce him. I mean, that's what probably led up to this, or added fuel to the fire anyway. But I don't know, I haven't talked to her. I think she's left the base already. She's got relatives close by, so she'll be fine."

Silence.

"Are you okay?"

"Kevin, you know he was drinking all the time. So don't go blaming it on her. If you drank like that, I would've left you a long time ago.

"No, no…that's not—"

I'm sorry. Really, I'm sorry. I didn't mean it that way." She stared out the kitchen window. "I just…I can't believe it went that far. Was he on drugs too, or something? I mean, why would he do that? Those poor recruits…"

"No, he wasn't on drugs. He just cracked. I wish I'd been there. Somebody should've been there. There were a couple DI's close by, but they just didn't catch on, I guess. Not in time, anyway…"

It was awkward. We'd finally gotten to a place where our smiles and touches were somewhat genuine again and we could be satisfactorily intimate when enough time had gone by, but clinging to each other during times of pain was taboo. That was my fault, I'm afraid. I didn't allow myself to reach out.

What happened to Drill Instructor Manso scared everybody. It took second only to the deadly Ribbon Creek march in terms of its horrific gash upon the reputation of Parris Island.

The balance had been tipped just a couple nights earlier. Manso had been driving home from an off-post bar when a cop pulled him over. He was tested, but only for procedure's sake, because his words were slurred and the smell of his breath indicated that his tolerance had been far exceeded.

So, a D.U.I. ticket was issued.

This is a big, big negative for a Marine. It can, and usually is, a deal-breaker. The general disposition of the hierarchy was to be intolerant of such tarnishing behaviors.

After being released into military custody, Manso was driven home and delivered to his wife, Sue, who grilled him about why he'd been out so late and any number or other things. Their marriage, too, had been rocky for some time, but nobody was sure which had come first, the chicken or the egg. Had problems conjured the drinking, or vice versa? Either way, he began to whine to her that his military career might be in jeopardy and I'm sure the whining entailed the castings of blame to the point that Sue became defensive; she then informed him that she hadn't loved him for years and that enough was enough. She was going to file for divorce, that very week.

I wish she'd timed things better, but nobody sees the underside of situations except God, so I'm not throwing stones. Sergeant Manso loved two things, the Corps and his wife, and the prospect of losing both brought him to a brink that was bound to collapse sooner or later. Sooner is just always so much harder to deal with.

The next morning Manso, dressed in pressed camouflage and wearing his gold DI buckle, duty-belt and cover, headed to the water training facility where he was serving a billet duty as a swimming instructor. His dress was odd because the normal uniform for that post was a t-shirt and shorts. As his students watched, he climbed the high dive ladder and seated himself at the end of the platform. He carried what looked like a rubber-training rifle and all the recruits were watching, wondering if he's really going to jump in with his DI cover on. It was a few minutes before anyone began to suspect this wasn't the beginning of some kind of strange training demonstration.

He sat down, letting his legs dangle from the platform, and threw his DI cover into the water below. That got their attention. A cover is a holy thing to a drill instructor, reverenced like the

American flag itself. A thing not typically flung around or treated casually.

His students sat solemn and transfixed as he put the muzzle of his rubber rifle under his chin and braced himself.

Then he pulled the trigger killing himself in front of those recruits and drill instructors waiting to start a day of training.

A word on military stress:

I remember how I felt the first time I stepped onto foreign soil. This is the last place I'll ever set foot, I had thought. Because, if you remember, Saddamm Hussein had threatened that the Gulf War would be the "Mother of All Wars." Though our nation and its defenders were confident, I think we still took the threat seriously and knew that anything was possible. Would they use chemical weapons on us? That day I accepted that I might die there and became okay with it. But the experience was stressful unlike anything I'd ever experienced. I carried a knot in my stomach that never left, day or night.

It's possible to wear stress, under the guise of strength, to the point that you become fragile. Rocks crack, after all, but fresh mud doesn't.

I think that's what happened to Manso, he failed to learn that it's the bending of a tree, not its rigidity, which keeps it intact through the storms. And, to be clear, these suggested shortcomings do not trouble the marine institute only, because they have to do with personal development issues that plague corporate and business environments as well.

I fall into the middle somewhere; I've never cracked but I am still to this day trying to learn to loosen up. I've paid a high price for the stresses I've endured and lost some things along the way that were unnecessary. Just gave some things up, doggone it. My heart goes out to this Marine and his family.

Dull Bayonets

Again, I'm not throwing stones, I'm just telling the story. I take full responsibility, as any Marine would, for the hardships my career imposed upon others.

For my wife and I, the years of my deployment sparked our decline.

The strain the Corps puts on a marriage during deployment and combat are sometimes hidden and ignored. Long periods of separation are like spaces between sentences—gaps that an occasional ten-minute phone call can't easily close. You forget where you left off so it's hard to start again. Things become awkward.

I'd call from a vessel somewhere in the pacific with the best of intentions, but my "how are you's" came out as a stiff salute and my "I love you's" became dull as backward bayonets. I'd try to hurry the calls along and my wife, in turn (sensing it) would do the same. That's how it starts, and your heart feels sad after each anemic conversation, but the adrenaline of life-in-motion draw you right back with its heady inertia.

I'm sad to say, out of pride, I never admitted to feeling those things. The discordant feelings. The tearing inside. I stowed my emotions in my duffle bag, hoping they'd show signs of life when I dredged them out for the next phone call, which never seemed to happen.

Our reunions, at least, were resuscitators; embraces always impart the sense of a better future and a touch is warmer than a transmitted voice. So, we'd rebuild our lives with fresh two-by-fours; we'd find new favorite restaurants and new fishing holes and reserve Tuesday nights for cards with our new friends and before we knew it, our two looked like one again, and even felt like it for the most part.

We had our good times, our sugar sprinkles, and though we're no longer together, acknowledging them helps us to be good friends to this day.

But new orders would eventually come, and we knew it.

On the one hand, I would relish it, because I didn't sit home well. On the other, I squirmed against having to fight off six or nine months of insecurity that comes with separation. My wife made friends easily and moved in and out of life's ordeals with such poise and liquidity that I envied her. She surrounded herself with free spirits—military wives and coworkers who shared her vibrancy. I mean, I was doing what I did best, and had had experiences that would seem cinematically exotic to most people but the grass is always greener on the other side, isn't it?

I'd sum it up this way: my wife lived life with her head tilted back in laughter while I lived it with a forced smile—a reliable tool that produced results I could count on. No surprises.

Island Life

When we landed on Parris Island and took up residence in our swamp patch, our world shrunk, which ended up being a good thing, as it forced us to look at each other and live with each other without escape routes. And, for all its swampy isolation, it was, well…kind of romantic in a Marine Drill Instructor kind of way.

My work took me long, but not far, and my wife kept herself fulfilled with a job in Beaufort. Our intersections may have been brief but they were daily, and as the outside world became more remote, our rare forays together took on an adventurous feel. I left my hurts under home soil where green, tended grass or pavement or concrete has a way of sealing over the broken shards of our histories.

"You know what?" I said one time.

"What?" she answered, checking the crockpot.

"I could stay here for the rest of my life, I think."

She gave me that look—the unreadable one that always kept me in suspense. "Oh yeah?" she said, turning to wipe the counter. "Let's wait and see what a hurricane feels like before we make that decision. You might not like it so much if you had to wade to work every day. Of course, the recruits would like it because you couldn't make 'em do pushups..." "Oh you better believe they would do pushups!"

Then she laughed, finding room for one more twist in her ponytail holder. She didn't like saggy, droopy hippie ponytails—they had to snap out so they'd bob with her jokes. "You'd build a boat, though, wouldn't you? Big enough for all your platoons and then make 'em clean it all day."

"Hey," I laughed. "Great idea! I'd build you and I a pilot house in it. With a deck and an observation dome. Maybe have a little margarita bar right next to the pilot's wheel."

"Oh, Mr. Imagination, huh? A pilot's house?" She cocked an eyebrow. "Sounds like a place where everybody sleeps at attention."

"He-he. No, my goal would be to put you 'at-ease.' And to keep you 'at-ease!'"

"Ohhhhh. That's your plan, is it? A lover's retreat, eh? Hey...wanna taste this?" She held out a big wooden spoon with a puddle of gumbo heaping at its edges.

I slurped at it then blinked with amazement as she told me she was pregnant.

"We're going to have a baby Marine?"

"Kevin..."

"Oh wow. Oh man. You're sure?"

"Yes, I'm sure. I've been to medical twice."

"Have you told anybody else?"

"Nope!"

I grabbed her and gave her a hug and she relaxed against my chest, the scent of her hair sweeter than any of the invading blooms that our back fence waged its unsuccessful war against.

"Let's call mom and dad," I said.

Feeling helpless

We knew the day was upon us and we had everything set to go but my wife was a toughie. She wasn't going anywhere unless it was absolutely necessary. A little bit of me—just a swab of my crust—must have rubbed off on her.

The night before we were supposed to check into the base hospital, her water broke while she sat on the toilet, but she was distracted enough that she didn't notice. She waddled back into the bedroom and lowered herself into as comfortable a drape as she could over a chair in the corner, positioning some pillows just so. Once propped, she'd be good for a couple hours of TV. She might even drift off between baby kicks and get some much needed rest, but the z's had been a rare oasis for her, so I didn't hold much hope for it.

She did remark that something felt different so she called the doctor and answered his questions to the best of our ability, but her information was vague. His best diagnosis suggested she sit tight and ride over in the morning. He'd be waiting, he informed her, raising his voice over a background of chatting nurses and buzzes and intercom alerts.

We got up early the next morning—drill instructor early—because Sergeant Flannery needed a ride to the barracks. So, at 0500, after giving myself a haircut, we were off. The splat of insects on our windshield annoyed me, as did Sergeant Flannery's well intentioned, but caffeine-fueled small talk. My wife was annoying me too. I had never felt so ill equipped and I was a man who knew about missions, so my ears were ringing and I felt light headed and coffee was doing me about as much good as a snort of baking soda. My wife was up front with me, but we were in no hurry, figuring everything was normal. We got Flannery to the barracks and he climbed out, wishing us an easy time of it before storming off to his awaiting herd like a rhino charging blind antelopes.

As we jostled back down the road I could hear him roaring, "Guide and squad leaders on my quarter deck, now…" His voice trailed away like the dust plume venting behind our car.

When we arrived at the hospital, life got fuzzy. The military did not write the book of efficiency, I realized. Hospitals did. The flashes of white were nurses and they seemed to know as much as the doctors did—this I surmised quickly. They wheeled my wife into a grey room and gathered around her so tightly all I could see was back and elbows as they pushed and prodded and acknowledged each other's decisions with crisp nods that served as approvals. These people knew their stuff and I became a fan.

One of the nurses informed the others, "She's dilated to eight," then, bending away from the mob at the waist until I was in her line of sight, she told me the same thing.

"Is that bad?" I asked?

"Sir, she is having her baby now."

I was speechless.

My authoritative DI voice had lost its power in this place. I don't know…maybe the sterile odors had affected my vocal cords, because everything I said sounded weak. So, I tossed my banal comments in here and there as I hovered nervously between the window and the birth team, reaching in whenever the sea parted to allow my wife to squeeze my arm during labor. I made a mental note: never let a woman enter the last week of pregnancy with long fingernails. The scars are still visible on my arms all these years later.

The same nurse threw another remark at me, "She had contractions all night, but just didn't know it," then leaned back in to her mysterious task.

Thirty minutes later, I heard my daughter's first disturbed, chattering cry, and was presented with hospital scissors, which I used to cut her lifeline. My wife and I would now be her lifeline and at that moment, I yielded my priorities, for the first time in my life, to a mandate that was of a higher and more strategic design than that given by a man of any rank.

Something in me surrendered, and I have not since tried to regain the lost territory of that stony ground and its narrow fighting holes.

I still had an "auto-pilot" button so recruits would never detect anything about me that didn't scream "drill instructor," but I knew deep inside right then that my days at Parris Island were numbered.

Change

Battle McDugle.

Sounds like a cartoon character, like "Beetle Bailey" or something. If we'd had a boy, who knows, maybe that would've been his nickname. I like the military ring of it, but then again, maybe it's too sing-songy.

But God gave us a girl, the most precious gift I've ever received. We named her Kylie Jordan and those two words rolled off our tongues like the way she made us feel—united. So we set about our task together, more a unit than we'd ever been, and learned as we went along.

I couldn't wait to get home. Life in the trailer didn't shut down so early as it used to. My wife would be up with Kylie feeding her or rocking her to stop a bout of fussing and although it was loud, our baby's cry had a pleasant sweetness to it that couldn't ruffle a cloud if it tried. I'd take her right away and my wife would totter, yawning, down the narrow hallway, groping for the wall like a blind man. I knew she was tired but she never complained. Not once. This was her new beginning too and she was as determined as I was not to screw it up.

As I held our little bundle on our sagging couch, awestruck by the beauty of her tiny details, my thoughts always went down the same uncluttered path: I cannot be a great dad and a great drill instructor at the same time. That was the sum of it. I'd never be home. My wife would burn out. She'd probably even get resentful and we'd fall right back into the stagnancy that had bound us for so long; and they both deserved all the provision I could sweat out and the fruits of all the strength I had.

The thought of leaving the Corps was scary—it was the only thing I'd ever been successful at, but I didn't want to miss a thing.

Grenade

"Come here," I said.

"Just a minute," my wife yelled from the back of the trailer. Her excuse for being late was always, "that darned cracked mirror in that dark ol' bathroom."

"Well, hurry…you gotta see this!"

I heard her moving up the hall. She stepped out into the dusty slice of evening light that our living room curtains had allowed to pass between their tattered edges. "What Kevin? I'm trying to get ready…"

"I know, but look…"

I had tucked Kylie into the bowl of my DI hat—she was a perfect fit!

"Oh Lord, we need a picture of that." She grabbed our Kodak and snapped away from a few different angles, murmuring as fresh mascara chunks blobbed the viewfinder and left her eyelashes not as evenly decorated as she would have liked. "Here," she said, handing me the camera. "I've got to finish getting ready. Take some more!"

Not too much later, she returned, tugging at some wrinkles in her skirt while eyeing me sideways. "Is that what you're going to wear?"

"Why…too casual?"

"Lose the tee and put on a polo shirt and you'll be perfect!"

"Okie-doke," I said. "Take Miss Muffet here and I'll be right back."

In the bedroom, I wrestled an aqua polo shirt over my shoulders and glanced in the dresser mirror. I'd been practicing not scowling. I'd spent so much time squinting my eyes and clenching my teeth, I found it difficult to present other expressions. It was probably false concern but I felt that way; I was very self-conscious about appearing harsh or even scary, now that I had a child.

Satisfied that I had arrayed myself with peace in a way that would make the angels proud, I rejoined my wife and Kylie, who had wet her diaper and was in the process of being undressed. A fresh one lay close at hand along with some moistened wipes and a rag. A clean jumper sat on the arm of the couch.

I tapped my foot against the trailer floor, restless to leave and with the knowledge that the diaper regiment was generally a quick procedure. I whistled a catcall and my wife glanced over her shoulder with a half-smile.

That's when it hit her.

Kylie completely uncorked, blowing everything her tiny body had stored in one explosive burst. The baby powder bottle blew over and the old wet diaper flopped open. Smelly half-solids of the type I wouldn't want to describe splattered everything within a six-foot radius of their source. Including my decked-out wife. Even the fresh jumper was contaminated. I was already running for rage but I wouldn't get any brownie points for it because I'd been out of the angle of fire and was still reprehensively clean. Evidently the back blast area was not secure.

I mopped and sponged silently while my wife rolled up her dress beginning at her knees and then lifted the wadded tube of clothing delicately over her head, dabbing her face and eyes with a clean corner of it.

My mind was running over jokes having to do with artillery shells and scorch-and-burn policies but I didn't have the bravery it took to launch humor at a half-naked woman with a bruised ego and who's tears were mingling with streaks of stuff that looked like it belonged on laboratory slides.

No, silence was the appropriate policy for the moment.

Well, except for my acknowledgement that I was volunteering for duty:

"Honey…just…just go and let me get it. You go change." I could not keep from laughing inside at my daughter and the smile on her face.

We were late that night, but fashionably so. We were both meticulous people so there was no clinging evidence to clue anyone into our personal environmental disaster. Nobody said anything, at least.

A new thing

We never argued. Neither one of us were confrontational. I could sure dish it out and I could take it on any kind of professional level but I hated to go back and forth about everyday life stuff. And my wife was the same way. I think that's what made the fluctuating phases of our coexistence endurable and even pleasant at times. We're genuinely nice people, if I may say so, and more the glass-half-full types than the other kind. And we understood each other, almost from the beginning, and never struck below the belt when we fought, which was as rare a thing in our marriage as a total eclipse. We just weren't that way. My prolonged absences, of course, prevented us from having the time even if we'd been predisposed to arguments.

You can tell someone loves you when they recognize your pain and aren't afraid or repelled by it. My wife's sensitivity proved that to me when our nation had one of its first encounters with an enemy that would become all too familiar: home-soil terrorism.

During an imposed two-month break (required of all drill instructors) I was assigned to a shop where plaques were made for DIs who were being reassigned or were retiring. Their covers are shellacked and mounted above brass plates with their name and rank on them, giving them a nice going-away present. The room I worked in was thick with the pleasant, if acrid, smell of solvents and paint and lacquers, and probably needed better ventilation, but I did my time easily and enjoyed the simplicity of my task. I hadn't really needed a break but oh well, why complain? And anyway, it gave me time to think about my wife and Kylie and our future. My daydreaming took on more substance and plausibility in those downtime reveries.

The office also had a small TV and one day I turned it on just in time to catch the news flashes about an explosion in Oklahoma City, Oklahoma. The Alfred P. Murrah building had been bombed, the very place I'd reported to at the beginning of my Marine journey. My stomach churned as the reporters detailed the damages and deaths; children had died, and babies. Office workers. And also… oh my God…several enlistees who's been in the MEPS (Marine Enlisted Processing Station) office. I knew one of the MEPS Captains stationed there. He told me later he'd stepped into a closet and when he turned back around his office and his poolies? were gone.

One hundred and sixty-eight people were killed altogether.

That evening my wife stayed on the phone with family and friends as the news chattered on about the devastation in the background.

The TV flickered for hours and I didn't move.

Gators

We didn't have a little wooden routed sign that said "The McDugles" screwed onto our aluminum door, nor did we have a mailbox. We picked up our mail at the base post office.

Nope. No identifiers. Heck, our trailer didn't even look Marine! But there we sat for two years, a speck in a swamp surrounded by other specks that were actually world-changers in green disguises—neighbors to alligators and legends and to the ocean itself. And we made a home of that trailer, breathed life into its aluminum pores with our words and our feelings and our love.

I wonder if the McDugle home still stands or if a hurricane has floated it away. It's been a long time. I think I'd prefer not to know and remember it just as I've described it to you.

But don't go looking for it now—there's gator's in them there woods!

McDugle, Flannery & Martin

Some of the hats I worked with were returning veterans, tough as beef jerky and just as meaty; often their skin looked like the terrain of the exotic foreign fields they'd served upon—creviced and cracked and of hues and shades that life on home soil couldn't produce. And though they'd seen lots, most of their experiences remained un-discussed because lodged memories, like broken-off bayonet points, cause less pain when un-tampered with. Their eyes still had sparks though, and their humor was like a fresh swig of canteen water on a blistering day.

In all likelihood, it was their humor that had seen them through their darkest days, dancing its laugh across rows of fallen comrades with just the right amount of homage while bracing their sanity with enough irony to preserve it.

That's what I think, at least.

I have seen death too and thought it horrendous, but the sun above the battlefields never stopped shining and the night skies never withheld their mocking horizons, so why should one allow himself to grow too serious?

Generally, a returning vet would do a cycle as a "heavy" then move straight to a Series Gunny spot, or some other senior position. A lot of them would've preferred to remain a heavy because it kept a person busy, but the decisions weren't always theirs. Evaluations were made above our rank and pay grades and we all had to accept the decisions.

I was out in the field one morning with one of these characters, a guy by the name of Merghardt. Gunnery Sergeant Merghardt. He was a crusty old Vietnam vet whose greatest weapon was his face. It had become so thick and plastery over time that it couldn't be read. Not even by me. I never knew what he was going to do next.

The day was off to a hot start and we had parked the recruits just out of reach of the shade of some big elms. A gentle breeze had stolen some cool air from the woods and was teasing the platoons with its leafy breath as they stood at attention, perfectly spaced and looking sharp.

That's when Gunny Merghardt started playing one of his favorite games.

He picked out a recruit that looked twitchy—maybe he had to go to the head or maybe he'd been bit up by sand fleas, who knows?—and got right up in his face. Then he grinned like a clown, bearing his yellow teeth, his bulbous, pitted nose turned up while he ogled the stoic recruit with his crazy eyes.

I could see the recruit doing his best to look through and past what had to be impossible to ignore. I'd seen this game before; if the recruit so much as flinched—if the corners of his mouth curled even the tiniest bit or if he allowed his eyes to dart and make contact that would be the end of his comfort for half a day.

I had to turn and choke back a chuckle of my own. This was rich.

The recruit did fine though; he must have had some supernatural inner reserve to draw upon, because Gunnery Merghardt's clown face evaporated and he stomped off to his next victim with a scowl. Same thing. He got within an inch of a dark green's face and produced his crazy expression. This guy couldn't maintain his composure, though. A snort belched through his nose, a little blast of air that drew attention to his quivering lips. The next thing I knew, the recruit was getting the chewing of his life by a guy I wouldn't want to meet in a dark alley. Or find myself in a trench opposite of.

It made for an interesting couple of hours. As a matter of fact, the rest of that cycle would have its curious moments.

Recruit Red

Around 1300 we sat the recruits down for chow, which would consist of MRE's (Meal, Read-to-Eat...a standard military ration) since we were in the field.

Now, I had one problem with MRE's—they contained gum and my recruits didn't need Popeye jaw muscles. And anyway, chewing gum was such a sloppy and unattractive habit that I didn't think any Marine should be caught dead chomping it.

So, I took off my soft cover and went from one to the next, collecting their little gum pellets before allowing them to consume their meals. And I'm a smart guy, so I knew to do a count afterwards.

If we had seventy-three recruits, I had better find seventy-three pellet packs in my cover. And I did. So chow time was uneventful except for the fire ants that had set up their own timeless perimeters and were defending their territory with aggressive versatility. There was a lot of boot stomping and leg swatting, but they weren't as bad as the sand fleas as long as you stayed clear of their nests.

Afterwards, the recruits fell in unusually fast, ready no doubt to march away from the infestation zone as quickly as possible, and I was of a mind to oblige them. A few of the toxic little troopers had managed to get under my socks somehow and I knew a good march would help us all to forget the tiny, red volcanoes that tormented our skin.

Unfortunately for the platoons, that's when I noticed Recruit "Red" (bright red hair adorned his freckled grape) grinding something in the moist lair of his mouth with practiced stealth.

"Recruit Red," I demanded, "come here. Didn't I tell you to give up your gum?"

"Sir, yes SIR!"

"Did you give it up?"

"Sir, yes SIR!"

I crossed my arms and riveted my eyes on his. "Then, where did you get the gum, Recruit Red? Were you storing it in your red butt kit?"

"Sir, no SIR! This recruit saved some yesterday and kept it in his pocket, sir!"

I looked him up and **down.** He was a sharp recruit in every way. He just needed some…habit breaking.

"Spit it into your hand, Recruit Red."

He did.

"Now, shove it up your right nostril," I ordered.

Then, a moment later—"FARTHER!" To my surprise, two trickles ran down his cheeks. Maybe the binding up of his nose hairs had damaged nerve endings near his eyes.

"Every time I see you for the rest of the day that gum better be in your nostril. Do you understand me?"

"Sir, yes SIR!" he shouted.

We marched away and rounded a sharp bend named "next" and if air was whistling through Red's blocked nostril, we couldn't hear it over our thundering cadence:

"Mamma mamma cant you see
What the corp has done to me
Cut my hair and shaved my face
Made me a part of the human race
Mamma mamma cant you see
See the sniper in the trees
Mamma mamma cant you see
He has his sites set on me
Mamma mamma cant you see
Your little boy may have to die
Mamma mamma cant you see
I killed the sniper in the trees
Wo wo woOO Wo wo **wow o**"

Staring at the paperwork

That night I stared at the paperwork and sighed. I would rather be jumping out of a plane. Or cleaning the head.

It just seemed endless. It was endless. Seventy some recruits meant seventy or so entries, night after night. Boring stuff too. So-and-so had a bruise on his left elbow…so-and-so was missing ten dollars from his money valuable bag. Recruit so-and-so hadn't received any mail in a week and was wondering if there was a glitch in the system.

I rattled my pen and let my mind wander.

There's a catfish in that little creek by the bridge on our road, I thought. I'd seen some big ol' tails swishing the surface of the water one morning, indicating they were either spawning or nesting. Gotta get a new pole.

Bored, and tired of the bitter bite of coffee (I'd had enough for the day) I strolled over to Staff Sergeant Martin's desk and stared impishly at his laptop. He'd bragged about coming up with a password nobody could guess and taunted us about the inviolability of his new machine.

Hmmm, I wondered. I know this guy pretty well. I know how that man thinks.

I sank onto the flimsy cushion of his chair and began to tinker. Sergeant Martin liked his alcohol, but not in a "lush" way…more of a connoisseur way. Well, maybe a hybrid of both; he was a renaissance man.

I began my password search. First, I typed in Jim Beam, Jack Daniels, Budweiser, and Coors Light. No luck, the little sign-in panel glowed resolutely, its blue pixels linking elbows against my fumbling intrusions. I got creative and tried more exotic titles: Stolichnaya, Vodgria Sangria and Guinness Stout. Access denied.

I grabbed a newspaper and searched until I found a liquor store ad and proceeded to go down the list, but to no avail.

Then, a flash of inspiration! I remember that he's always touted the virtues of a certain drink he'd discovered overseas and become fond of, a concoction that seldom showed up on menu's and had to be specifically requested: Mojo!

In a flash, I was in!

Yeah, yeah, yeah…I know you, old man.

I didn't snoop around his files. That would've been dirty and backstabbing. The victory was in knowing a friend so well that you could navigate his barricades and scale his highest walls. Not that picking his lock had been that difficult. Mojo?

That should've been my first try.

I gave him crap about it for days, but I think he kept the password anyway. We were all tight. Our little crew of recruit-thumpers, had shared the bad and the good with each other in sometimes unnecessarily explicit detail, so there were no trust issues. And that's how it should be and was, for the most part. Occasionally there would be the odd guy who wanted to cut his own swath, but I experienced that infrequently.

And I consider myself blessed for it.

On the subject of Staff Sergeant Martin, I want to reiterate my opinion of the man. He was one of the best senior DIs I ever had the privilege to work with because he understood his role and had no private agenda wagging its "stroke me" tail behind it.

A senior's job is to become the recruits' "daddy" figure. At times, he'll remove his cover when he addresses them, something the rest of us never do, and listen to their concerns with genuine interest and compassion. He wouldn't coddle them—he absolutely refused to and would shut down in a heartbeat if he sensed manipulation or self-pity—he earned their respect through raw honesty. He was as hardcore as any of the other DIs on our team, yet he loved his platoons and the men that populated them. He became a base favorite - an intimidating one, but a favorite nonetheless.

As a result, our cycles together generated some of the best-trained Marines ever released to the fleet marine force.

Bad DI

There was a downside though, to the relentless commitment our team gave to the recruits. As I've discussed before, relationships suffer tremendously from the grueling hours, and the damage isn't undone by watching a half hour TV show with your loved one in the evening or by having a ten-minute conversation before bed.

Senior DI Staff Sergeant Martin and Sergeant Flannery both lost wives and girlfriends, which tore me up. Staff Sergeant Martin had loved his LBFM (little brown female, a beautiful Pilipino who kept him in line) and it broke his heart when they split.

They couldn't be blamed though. They felt tolerated rather than loved, as their time allowances were slotted like lunch breaks - later at night than normal people usually stay awake.

Who could live that way?

Who could live with people with nicknames like "Sergeant Satan?"

Sergeant Flannery had been nicknamed "Sgt. Satan" by the recruits because he was a force to be reckoned with; he was lean as a welterweight but tough…he'd knock a rifle butt into the back of a recruit's head in a second if he thought it would make a better Marine out of him. He had a raw face with protruding jawbones and was a downright scary fellow, even when he wasn't shouting. But I knew the guy beneath the horns; he had feelings, felt loss, was smart, loved the Corps and had dreams beyond the Corps—things he wanted to do with his future after he'd done his time and felt a release to move on. He was a fine man, just disoriented like all of us by the weight of our assignments.

I don't want to make us sound like martyrs, or like social misfits, but sometimes it felt like all we had was each other. If any one of my co-workers had done anything wrong, I would've covered for them, but I never had to. They were men of integrity. I'd measure them up against all others.

One time a DI from another platoon (it was a small green world so nothing took place in a corner) collected money from his recruits for a pizza party. At least, that's what his story was. He ended up spending the money partying, to the embarrassment of our battalion's officers. He was removed quickly, given NJP (Non-judicial Punishment), and reassigned to—well, I don't know where—probably to Antarctica or something.

I've said it before, that type of behavior and irresponsibility is rare in the Corps, and particularly among drill instructor ranks, but incidents occasionally mushroom into the light.

I never witnessed criminality first hand.

I never had to cover for anything that would've prickled at my conscience.

Girls in covers

During one of the least stressful periods in my remembrance (the stabilizers seemed to be operational in all of our non-military relationships), Senior DI Staff Sergeant Martin, Sergeant Flannery and I sat down to debate a base hot topic. The recruits were lined up like two-by-fours on top of the tightly made racks and were already snoring. We didn't feel like going home yet, so our discussion began over Styrofoam cups of reheated java.

"Whaddya think about the female DIs being allowed to wear campaign covers?" Sergeant Flannery asked, sucking air over his burnt tongue and dabbing a napkin to the darkening spots on his collar.

"Nope. Nope-nope-nope," said Staff Sergeant Martin. "Can you see that on a woman? It'll make 'em all look like men!"

"He-he," I chuckled. "That would be a sight! Slim bodies under a big cover, it just doesn't seem right, does it? It goes against tradition in a way that doesn't sit right with me."

"Yeah, and it's never been an issue before! Why NOW?" Staff Sergeant Martin stretched his legs and crossed them. "Ah well. They're gonna do what they're gonna do. The brass likes everything to look consistent and that's probably what's got into their grapes. And..." he paused to blow on his coffee, "maybe they think it'll make for better publicity photographs and encourage more young women to enlist."

"They're probably right," said Flannery.

I was a traditionalist so I held my tongue as I sensed their general neutrality on the issue.

I had an enormous respect for female DI's. They're a unique breed. Some are pretty and some are plain but the garnishments of a Marine uniform and the shine of an un-stainable character beautifies them all - you can't not notice one walking by. They project a possessiveness that takes ownership of everything within their personal radius, and no matter how lovely their eyes might be they're actually scanners connected to lightning-fast computers.

I knew quite a few of them and they were sharp. There's not a lot of intermingling. At Parris Island, males are separated from females at the boot camp level; they never bump into each other and only rarely catch glimpses of one another's platoons.

And the gals train hard...my goodness!

The curriculum for female recruits is exactly the same as the men's; some of the physical requirements are eased as far as repetitions are concerned, but not in form.

They have to qualify on the same obstacle course and on the same rifle range and under the same field conditions as the guys do; no slack. So you can imagine how tough a female DI is repeating their personal training between every recruit cycle - just like the rest of us, time after time after time.

Flannery cocked a fuzzy, thick eyebrow; "Ya know," he chuckled, "they say the last thing you wanna run into on a bad day is a drill instructor. I think the last thing you wanna run into is a female DI on her monthly…!"

We snorted how true that probably was and slurped from our steaming cups.

"Wait," I said. "I think the female DIs are trained to stay on their monthly until the end of their cycles. Maybe that's why they're so mean!"

"Maybe that's why they're so doggone charming between cycles!'

Traveling

"It's not so much that they're cheap," I told my wife. "I see it as placing responsibility?"

She stretched her "okaaaaay" - its exaggeration was firmly emphasized.

I understood though. Our income was moderate, even with both of us working, so we had to handle our finances with practicality. I needed a new uniform for an upcoming trip and they weren't cheap. And they weren't handed out upon request either.

The Marine Corps is the only branch of service that requires their marines purchase their own uniforms. Every time you see a marine wear camouflage, you're seeing where part of his paycheck went. The same goes for his dress blues and his boots. In fact, when a recruit graduates from boot camp, everything he's acquired up to that point is deducted from his paycheck—and it amounts to a pretty hefty chunk.

I owned a sword that I could wear with my dress blues, but I had to purchase it. I owned two pairs of jump boots and had scrimped and saved for the second. The same is true with my DI covers. I don't think I ever owned more than two at a time, but that was plenty because we'd been taught how to scrub them out, wash them off and even had small presses that would keep the rims hard and flat. Also, Scotch-Guard and starch, that heavenly-inspired formula, extended their lifespan with repeated treatments.

They didn't last forever though.

Now you know why a drill instructor's eyes are popping when a recruit's at the end of a round of push-ups and his cover is beneath him. "You better not squash my cover, recruit! You better stay up on those arms…!"

I never had one fall, not once!

"How long will you be gone?" my wife asked.

"Mmmm, three days I think. I'll fly in Tuesday night, spend most of Wednesday at the recruiting office and then leave Thursday morning. Long trip. I've got a two-hour layover in Chicago."

Kylie was scooching across the carpet with a pacifier half in - half out of her mouth, trying to use the floor to leverage it back into place.

"Is Sweetwater going to be there?"

"I don't know yet. But if I see Jennifer, I'll tell her you said hi!"

"Tell her to call me. It's been over a year."

I loved the excursions to recruiting offices; they were nice changes of pace that didn't break up my "DI flow." Recruiters liked to have real DIs come and speak to their poolies (civilians who'd already enlisted but hadn't shipped out yet) and tell them the good, the bad and the ugly—just what they could expect from their upcoming boot camp experience. The recruiter's philosophy was that it would reduce the initial "fog of war" stress, (as we liked to call our intense, in-your-face introductions), while showing to the poolies that drill instructors could be congenial and affable outside of their training personas.

So, I'd talk to the poolies for a while and share some stories, then, after a warning, I'd gun my engine and yell at them for a few minutes. It was a lot of fun and I enjoyed assisting the recruiters as they helped those young and eager men and women prepare for their Marine futures. It was nice to not have to be "on" every second.

They only got a glimpse of the real Sergeant Death, though. If I had unleashed to the full extent, nobody would've reported for training at Parris Island!

That particular trip was a huge success. I was impressed with the caliber of young people the recruiters had assembled and even enjoyed a few jokes with them. Not one seemed cavalier or inattentive, or like he was running from something. They genuinely wanted to shine, and it showed!

I bragged on them to my wife when I returned.

"Man, you shoulda seen those kids," I remarked, as the river lapped at its thirsty edge not far from our Plum's table? "They all have it in 'em, they're going to make outstanding marines."

"Oh, that's great," she said. "Sometimes I worry about our next generation of young people. I'm so glad MTV hasn't whacked 'em all out!" She stuck her tongue in the concave of an ice cube and slurped at me, "Now, can we dance?"

Swordplay

Drill instructor school was tough on purpose. A lot of guys didn't make it through and that was well and good; if you weren't cut out for it, you weren't cut out for it! But there were always a few that made it that I didn't think should have. They handled the physical stuff okay, but didn't seem to possess the x-factor that commanded attention effortlessly. One in particular really grated on me, but out of respect, I'm going to change his name for the following narration; I'll call him Schmoe.

"Sergeant McDugle, would you go around and gather all the record books for graduation?" Senior Drill Instructor Staff Sergeant "Schmoe" had been a marine postal clerk before becoming a DI. But now, he was my senior, my boss. He was likeable enough, but had a weak vocal endowment. His bookish leadership kept the word of the Corps perfectly but didn't embody the spirit of it. He was just missing something that his position required. And besides that, we weren't well suited personally. When he spoke to me, voltage didn't fly through my wiring. In fact, the opposite occurred. It was like flint striking stone—sparks flew.

"Sure, I sure will," I answered, thinking how much I missed Staff Sergeant Martin. The Marines move people around and we all had to accept it.

So, I went to administration, dental and medical and made my way around the base until I'd gathered all the paperwork on our recruits. I had their SRB (Service Record book) medical and dental records—everything.

I had paid extra attention to the details and triple-checked every record to insure I had them in my possession. I knew the routine. I turned over the box of records to Staff Sergeant Schmoe and told him to make sure to pass them out by the numbers because recruits tended to screw the process up every time.

The next day, Staff Sergeant Schmoe called me back into the squad bay office, where he proceeded to light into me with a pinched sneer and nasally bursts of reprimands. Coming from another Senior, who knew how to lay things out in a row and put them back together with just, if stern, dignity, I would've acquiesced. But he was telling me that I hadn't done my job and that I'd obviously lost some very important material.

"Now, listen," I said, "last night I handed you a box with every record book in it. I crossed 'em all off myself."

"No, you couldn't have," Staff Sergeant Schmoe said, "if you had picked up every record book, every recruit would have their record and as of now, we are missing one."

"Are you calling me a liar? Don't you go questioning my integrity"

It went back and forth, becoming more heated as the words flew, and that would've been fine if it hadn't been for the constant insinuations pertaining to my integrity. That was the straw that broke this green camel's back and wrought a new and legendary base anecdote, one that I'm sure is still recited today, maybe as cadence, but surely with the colorful details that years add on to any good story.

I had my dress blues on because we'd been practicing for Friday's graduation ceremony, which meant I had my sword too. Swishhhhh! Out it came as I leaped onto the big wooden desk in the center of the room. I drew it back in preparation to plunge it into his chest. His eyes were as big as saucers and his face was red.

Before I knew it, two other DI's had grabbed me from behind and were dragging me off the desk, but I could see through the porthole in the separating wall that all of the recruits had observed the interrogation, including my three musketeer routine.

I was still upset and continued to holler at Staff Sergeant Schmoe as they shouldered me out of the room, "I'll find those stinking books! If it takes all day I'll find them!" He was furious, but shaken and remained silent.

Well, I did find the missing books and paperwork, wedged in between the pages of another recruit's who hadn't taken the time to skim through it completely.

In the end, I salvaged my integrity, and thanks to two other DI's I stayed out of the brig. I realized at that time that I needed to work on some inner patience issues of my own. Some adjustments needed to be made. I loved being a cannon but the Marines didn't need a loose one.

I couldn't stand weak marines, especially those who blamed others for their mistakes. I believe I grew from that episode. And Staff Sergeant Schmoe—that was his last cycle as a drill instructor (by choice). He moved on and took another position somewhere else where I'm sure he does his country proud.

I still have my sword. I paid a lot for it, though it's only been pulled once, I keep it close by!

Time to go?

I regretted the breakup of McDugle, Flannery, and Martin—it had been a great team. But change is a bittersweet fact of life. It's unavoidable. I worked with those guys for several more cycles and remained friends for long afterwards, but nothing ever seemed quite the same.

That's the downside of the military. People come and people go. Recruits come and go.

Glancing down at Kylie as she slept in my lap, I realized that a recurring thought had become as regular as tracers in a rifle's magazine: Maybe it was time for me to go.

It scared me to death.

I didn't know how to do anything else.

"Mr." McDugle, Civilian

When the ferns browned, toward the end of my second year at Parris Island, fall was approaching on turbulent grey waves. I began to take seriously the unshakeable feeling that a chapter in my life was about to close. Don't misunderstand...I was still sharp as a Gillette razor and the timing of my cadence was always spot-on; my problem was, I was losing a heart-battle. In all fairness, I couldn't let my family limp along another mile in the condition we were in. They deserved better.

So did the recruits if I couldn't give them 100% of myself. My best friend told me I should concentrate and treat my wife like a queen - I had a long way to go.

The recruits in my present cycle were terrific. Their twelve weeks had passed by in a blur. Suddenly, there I was, standing before them on a blustery morning, blinking sand out of my tired eyes as I considered how eager they looked.

And though I wasn't one to show it, a celebratory atmosphere had taken a hold of everybody, the brass included, as the cooling temperatures relieved our baked brains.

Graduation day at Parris Island is always a memorable experience. The weasels that had irritated me so much during their first intrepid weeks were not weasels anymore. They were stout young champions preparing for their initiation into an elite and rare brotherhood that only claimed a couple hundred thousand active members worldwide at any given time. The Marines are the smallest of the United State's armed forces, so there's a camaraderie that displaces previous alliances, a pride that elevates our chins to the same height. Once a Marine, always a Marine.

But for all the satisfaction I felt at having accomplished the near impossible, I always found graduation to be a gooey experience. I never liked it…the tears and the "thank yous" and having to meet all the parents. Remember, my mind was on the weekend and the few days of down time I'd hopefully get before the next cycle swept in. So trying to play a different role—that of a friendly good-guy-after-all type made me edgy.

Once I got in trouble when a recruit I didn't particularly care for got approved to graduate after I'd warned my superiors concerning him barely qualifying. His parents came to my table the night before dabbing their eyes with tissues. I cut off their thank you in mid-sentence and informed them that I didn't believe their son was qualified for marine service and if it had been up to me, he wouldn't be graduating - however he'd met the basic requirements and was being allowed to slip through a paper crack. Later, my Series Commander pulled me aside and warned me about talking to parents like that. I was disgruntled to say the least, but oh well…I hope the young man lived through his assignment on foreign soil.

I didn't like the awkward silence, either. After all, I'd spent twelve weeks teaching the recruits to respect the DI to a high degree. Now they didn't have to call me "sir" ("sergeant" was acceptable) and this somehow deemed it appropriate to lunge at me on the parade deck, snot running down their tear-streaked hardened faces as they said "thank you" with a hug.

You get the picture.

Some parents even offered me money.

Personally, I felt a handshake was more than appropriate; it was the manly thing, and appropriate for a Marine. Anything more than that was an invasion of my personal space or would have been if I hadn't been marine property. I know that the ceremonies and the emotions were all in the line of duty and I enjoyed, more than life itself, training these boys to become men.

During any graduation, I was keenly aware of the thousands of DIs who had gone before me, setting an awfully high but attainable standard; I know in my heart I did my best, my very best, and that I had been a hard taskmaster to bear; I had allowed NO TV breaks, and no treats. No extra sleep, no pats on the back. When my recruits left my care, they were ready for the next level of training and for the mental anguish that the fog of war would throw at them.

With a few exceptions, they had not just endured and made it through by the skin of their teeth; they had earned the title of U.S. Marine. Not one of them would wonder if he'd been given some kind of special grace along the way - if some weakness had been overlooked. Nope. There had been no grace. Just hard, hard work.

So, there I stood, that last cycle, blinking the dust out of my eyes and feeling as grey as a wave on the inside as I recalled the torment I'd endured for the past twelve weeks. You see, since becoming a marine, fear had been driven from me—I'd forgotten what it even felt like.

But a recurring thought had opened the door to it again, starting a war in my emotions that spilled out at home as resentment, bitterness, and built up irritation. That thought was this: would I make it "out there?"

The thought of leaving the only thing I'd ever been good at made my stomach wrench. Tough as I was, I realized that an integral part of life's growth process had been handled for me by the marines; they had made all of my hardest decisions for me. You see, as a marine, you are told where to be and when to be there, and all you have to do is follow orders and show up. In fact, the easiest thing to do at my present crossroad would be to re-enlist. I found great comfort in the simplicity of service.

So, how would I support my family if I left, I wondered? Could I succeed as a civilian, or would I flounder?

Before joining the Corps, I had spent a short time working as an electrician in my father's business but I had never mastered the calculations and methodology of that industry. Plus, a considerable amount of time had passed and technology had changed the entire landscape of the electrical field; it would be like starting over. After a lot of contemplation, I realized I didn't have the heart **or** the passion to start the learning process from scratch.

For a while, I considered becoming a police officer, but were my motives right? Was I just looking for another service-type job where the duties were procedural and where the dress code was a uniform? Later, I actually filled out some applications, but a door never opened. Good thing; I'm not sure the hours and responsibilities of a beat-cop would've met the conditions for change I'd envisioned for my family.

McDugle, all your fears and mental wrangling are wasted energy at this point, I told myself. *You've already signed on the dotted line, anyway…*

The first recruits had been called and were filing forward, bright eyed and excited, but inwardly I was trembling slightly as I shook their hands. That very week I'd made my move and turned in my paperwork.

I would be leaving the Corps.

I smiled at the other DIs on the platform, but their smiles in return were wistful and forced. I'd never done anything so hard, painful, questionable, scary…

Adjustment

The following Monday I was a civilian. What a shock to the system! Everything moved in slow motion back in Oklahoma - where I was just another guy getting his oil changed or picking up a quart of milk at a convenience store. My haircut and grouchy face apparently were not enough to signal who I'd recently been. Where was the respect?

Nothing seemed clean and nothing seemed organized. The world was permeated by odors I'd forgotten, and was gritty and grimy and had potholes on every corner. Un-mowed lawns irritated me, so I'd grumble under my breath about my neighbors. I had to bite my tongue to not chew people out. So what if their driveways had oil stains? Their priorities were obviously different than mine.

My wife sensed my uneasiness, and related to it - I think. After all, her life in my shadow had been an ordered one. Although the transitions weren't as difficult for her, it still required some adapting. She had to re-learn how to make small talk, how to stand in long checkout lines, how to make new friends. In the military a marine's orders pretty much determine the inner circle of your life - whether you like them or not. You may have off-post acquaintances, however inside you can't shake the feeling of fraternizing with foreigners. That's both a good thing and a bad. It's good because it strengthens the Corps, but it's bad in that it creates a sense of distance from the rest of the world.

Another thing I found extremely difficult was being around my wife all day. I confess I felt a bit lost. I was still sleeping only two to four hours a night (it would take a few years for my sleep cycle to return to normal). That left me twenty hours every day. Hours I had the hardest time filling them with substitutes for the adrenaline rush I was used to. Nothing adequately filled the void.

I believe that's when I began to think differently, and to think more. I had to get creative or I would go nuts.

One of the first things I did was to join a National Guard recon unit. Old habits are hard to break, and I thought I needed a military "methadone," to slowly wean me from the extreme disciplines of structure. I'll write another book about that experience. It was like throwing a hand grenade into a fighting hole; I was too mean, too wound up, and too biased to settle for the more lax expectations of that well-intended organization.

My first job was for a software company in Stillwater, Oklahoma. I can't say that I loved that period or that job in particular, but it was necessary.

My social skills had to be refined and I had to develop some new skill sets, ones that hopefully would compliment my sturdy personality. I also enrolled in some classes at Oklahoma State University. I may have felt out of my element as I took all of these awkward steps, but I was never afraid. I waded in like they were creeks in a South Carolina bayou. They were nothing more than just little bitty challenges.

That job was pivotal (so I'm grateful) as it led to jobs with tech-related corporations - corporations providing products and services to Fortune 500 companies around the world. My horizons were broadening!

Along the way, another creative idea sprung to life in my increasingly busy mind: I was 27 by that point and needed some money to close on a house, so I started a side business, a physical fitness boot camp that would keep me as active as I wanted to be and also benefit others. It was a three-week program based around an hour-a-day of calisthenics, swimming, and running. Now, that turned out to be a romping success! The Stillwater newspaper ran a story on my upcoming effort, so my first class boasted 75 students. All of them were civilians and most had never accomplished what they had hoped to in life. It was a perfect match!

The idea channeled what came so naturally to me, discipline and endurance into a thriving venture. I made a lot of new friends and connections in the process. I didn't realize it at the time, but that simple step-of-faith was a pivotal move in my life, as it bolstered my waning confidence and taught me that focus and integrity where character traits that integrated well into the self-employed arena. My ability to multi-task and follow through also contributed highly to that initial success. I was very dedicated to whatever I threw myself into.

Plus, I still got to be a drill instructor, albeit a semi-nice one. I'm particularly proud of one of my routines: I would take my class into the deep end of a swimming pool, where they had to tread water, and have them form a circle. Then, I would produce a brick which each had to hold above his or her head for sixty-seconds before passing it to his neighbor, who, after doing to same, would pass it to the next. Slowly, that brick would make its way around the circle as I taught survival skills and other subjects. After the last person held up the brick for the specified time, I would make my point: "If I had told you before we started that each of you were going to tread water for an hour, many of you would've panicked in the first five minutes. But I've kept your minds busy with a task and some stories. You've accomplished almost effortlessly what might have seemed a daunting prospect. Your body has the ability to run marathons, swim oceans, hike the tallest mountains and fulfill ambitions if you can overcome the mental barriers that block the way. This goes for personal goals, physical goals, business goals—anything! If you set your mind to it…you can do it!"

Teaching those folks without having to worry about making marines out of them helped me relate to everyday people in a fresh, new way. I learned to love people for who they were and to accept their imperfections. Those were fun times, as well as growing times. My best friend and I finally connected again and started a new relationship that was much deeper than before.

In the years following, as I re-wired my mind to civilian life and learned its ins-and-outs, I started several businesses and invented a number of successful products. It was as though a switch had been turned on; I wasn't just a fighting machine or a war robot. Creative gears were turning inside of me and, although not everything turned to gold (I made some mistakes), I found I was better at normal life than my initial fears had hinted at.

I thank God, for I believe that through the good and the bad, His hand has been on me. His plan is unfolding.

Yes, everything was going great and my insecurities were slowly dissolving, but on the home front, the years of strain were beginning to take their toll. I don't think my wife or I did anything wrong after leaving Parris Island—I just think the wide spaces that our new lifestyle brought us made room for pre-existing issues to surface. Strong as I was, in regard to our relationship, I had no fight left in me, and my wife felt the same way. It had been a long haul and we were both exhausted.

It doesn't matter how it all went down; suffice to say that we were equal and amiable and shed bittersweet tears together as we ended our marriage and said goodbye. We would remain close, and had Kylie as proof that we had not been completely fruitless, as we'd made our way through those tough, tough years. Something very precious had come out of our struggles.

Let me just add, that although I miss the camaraderie of the Corps to this day, I will never regret being able to help guide my daughter to adulthood. As of the writing of this book, she is nearing her high school graduation and I am so proud of the young lady she's become. I smile when I think about this: a few years back, she was going through a tough time and I asked her if she was going to be okay; she replied, "Dad, I have marine blood in me. I will always be okay!"

Feeling helpless

In 2001 I hit a low point, the only really bottoming out that I've experienced since my Marine Corps departure. I found myself depressed watching coverage of the 911 twin tower attacks on the news.

I felt like I should be overseas helping the men I trained to fight - leading them.

It was hard to sit on the sidelines while others put their life on the line for my freedom. That was the hardest pill I have ever had to swallow. I know my dad was of the same cloth, when the first Gulf War started and I received my orders my dad went to the recruiting station and requested they take him at 52 years of age. I love his heart and willingness to give all.

Onwards

As I continued to grow my businesses, I found that I got exceptionally excited when a former marine sat across from me with a job application. They carry a winner's attitude and have developed the character needed to forge through any difficulty. As Clint Eastwood puts it, they know how to "improvise, adapt, and overcome." Those are the traits that balance the scale when you're not the best at something. I personally wasn't the best marine in the corps. I was simply one of those guys who would charge through hell with a water pistol if I were ordered to do so. I was no longer a quitter.

In 2011, I had the privilege of meeting John Maxwell, a true leader, an author, speaker, and pastor who had written more than 60 books. What a thrill! What an unforeseen advent! If you had told me when I was young what my future would hold, I would have been astounded to know the caliber of people I would cross paths with. When John and I met he said as he often does, "Hi, I'm John and I am your friend." I was honored to become a founding partner of the John Maxwell Team. I became a certified coach, speaker, and trainer for his esteemed organization, and gained invaluable insights from the close fellowship I experienced during that time. I love the fact that John is a man of his word and a man who follows God in all he does. Simply put, John taught me it is important to love people in all you do. He will hopefully one day read this book and smile with warm humor at the transparency of my life today compared to my former crusty demeanor (a side no one in my present life has seen). Please remember that this book is not about the finest of Marine leaders; it is my experience and the mistakes I made. I was something, wasn't I, John?

Boys…so many years have passed. I feel like I'm just getting started though.

I currently own two businesses: Lawyer Marketing Services and eXpect3 Marketing; I have also been developing a number of products which should be available by the time this book is released. One of my proudest activities is to be the Executive Director of Soldier's Wish. We get to grant wishes all across the country for the men and women who are serving or have served this great nation. Please visit www.soldierswish.org to learn more.

Thank you so much for spending time with me. I hope you enjoyed a look behind the scenes at a Marine Corps training facility and into the life of one of its former residents. Let me say goodbye to you with the acknowledgement of a few personal heroes:

Thank you to: Colonel Oliver North, Commandant of the Marine Corps, General Al Grey, and the countless other Marines who stood and currently stand in defense of this nation - the greatest nation on the face of the earth. I am proud to have had the opportunity to call myself a Marine, One of the Few and the Very Proud—proud of all those Marines that came before me, those I served with, and those who will become Marines. "Semper Fi" and God bless.

I had several mentions in this book about my best friend but I failed to introduce him to you. You can read more about him on the website. Also, on the website you can leave your boot camp stories and videos as long as it is kept clean. My best friend's name is Jesus and he is the leader of all leaders. He has cleaned up my language and made me whole. The Bible says "a greater love has no man than this; that he lay down his life for his friends."

Kevin McDugle
DI SGT USMC
April, 2013